AMERICA
VS
AMERICANS

HOW CAPITALISM HAS
FAILED A CAPITALIST NATION AND
WHAT WE CAN DO ABOUT IT

· ·

ERIC WADE
WITH PHIL HEREL

Forefront
BOOKS

. . . .

FOR ADAM SMITH, whose book
An Inquiry into the Nature and
Causes of the Wealth of Nations
helped lift millions of people
(including the author himself) out of poverty.

Rest now, our dear friend . . .
peaceful in the knowledge American Laborism
will take care of the people you couldn't.

. . . .

CONTENTS

PREFACE

THIS IS A CONVERSATION about American Laborism.

This has nothing to do with the Labor Movement, organized labor, the British Labour Party, or *going into* labor.

American Laborism is a new economic system for managing the entire US and therefore a replacement for capitalism.

American Laborism respects *labor* in the way that capitalism respects *capital*.

Labor is in turn respectful of the individual in ways that capital never could be. Capitalism may seem American but is clearly not in the best interest of all Americans.

Capitalism has its merits. But it also has shortcomings, which most obviously led to where we are today, with the largest wealth inequality gap in American history.

It is the goal of American Laborism to fix that.

Therefore, this book is for workable, low-tax capitalism for those who want it and a dignified, healthy, happy, and fulfilled life for everyone at the very least.

I hope to introduce you to an economic system that may sometimes feel familiar and yet also challenges you to believe it is still a dream that could be possible.

I predict that the readers of this book will almost immediately self-segregate into two camps: those who are sure this is an impossible, silly, overly simplistic economic dream, and those who see common sense and perhaps merit in these pages, along with hope for a fair, prosperous, and peaceful future.

Even though this book is meant as an introduction to a new economic framework (which ordinarily would be expected to appeal to a highly educated audience), in this case the ideas are more geared for readers with little to no formal economic background or education.

Readers, however, who *do* have common sense.

That's simply because American Laborism, as you'll see, is a simple, unassuming, uncomplicated framework that any society could immediately implement. In fact, it's so simple that I've laid out everything you need to know in chapter 1. It is this chapter that will make sense to ordinary people.

Who are these ordinary people? Folks who know the value of their own labor and are willing to accept that everyone else's labor has value too.

However, ordinary people are no longer able to influence policy or determine what rules they'll live under, and they are woefully unlikely to regain these luxuries any time soon. Therefore it's necessary to expend numerous further chapters rebutting the "intelligent" arguments undoubtedly held by people who will bemoan the unfairness, poverty, and inequality inherent in our *present* system while simultaneously adding power to that same system.

It is those people, the most powerful and the best educated, who will, I'm certain, require seventy thousand words to understand what ordinary people will grasp in fewer than two thousand words of chapter 1.

In other words, this book will make sense to people who have common sense . . . and it will anger, annoy, and befuddle people who believe themselves to have *uncommon* sense.

So be it.

Read this book with a mind willing to accept that we, as Americans, can have everything we want, while simultaneously ensuring that we all—even the least among us—live dignified, meaningful lives. The answer is here. It's not just possible; it's easy.

Before I present the succinct explanation of American Laborism *and* the longer explanation for those who can't accept how simple it is, I feel it's important to make something clear.

I'll explain American Laborism in the context of life in the United States of America. This is simply because I believe America can do this, and frankly, I believe America desperately needs it. If a sufficiently brave politician stepped forth to lead America through the transition to American Laborism, it could be achieved as quickly as laws could be written and regulations changed. As of now, America is not working for Americans.

Sadly, reducing regulations is not something that America can implement immediately without a monumental change like American Laborism, as we are a country that has lately begun to favor bloated laws and immense numbers of regulations. But when I say Laborism *could* be implemented quickly, I believe it really could be.

After America adopts Laborism, there is no reason that the rest of the world wouldn't immediately follow. And frankly, I would expect that to be extremely rapid, because as you'll see, Laborism would make America so much more efficient, competitive, educated, militarily strong, and low-taxed that no country in the world could compete with it. Their only hope to retain their best, brightest, and hardest-working citizens would be to switch to Laborism themselves.

That is not an outrageous claim!

American Laborism will soon provide the following benefits:

- Low taxes
- Unlimited, lifelong education
- A strong military
- Zero involuntary homelessness, starvation, or malnutrition
- A sound currency, backed by assets such as gold

Most importantly, Laborism will enjoy enthusiastic participation by all citizens of America, be they rich or poor, young or old, liberal or conservative.

American Laborism isn't just a replacement for capitalism. It's an upgrade. Every human has the right to live a life of dignity, to contribute, and to ensure that their basic needs are respected by their society.

I've made a great living under capitalism . . . but it has failed us.

American Laborism, however, can improve the lives of every member of our society by bringing upward the least among us *without bringing down anyone else.*

And when I say that, I mean it locally, nationally, and globally. I'll go into more detail in later chapters. And again, if you find all this impossible to believe, I think chapters 2–15 can convince you.

INTRODUCTION

I'VE BEEN CONTEMPLATING American Laborism for years. Like many authors, I started and stopped writing numerous times. Fortunately, every time I stopped, I was presented with an opportunity to gather deeper insight and challenge my own ideas.

But simultaneously, I grew ever more frustrated with myself and this unfinished idea because millions of people will live better lives if we are bold enough to attempt the simple idea shared in these pages.

And then I had the good fortune to meet a brilliant young man who, as we became friends, I discovered asks great questions, has a keen mind, is a fast learner, and possesses endless curiosity.

I decided if we could just have a conversation about Laborism, and if I noted his thoughts and questions, the rest would take care of itself.

That's what this book is, as much as possible. Indeed, we had what I recall to be a good conversation about what American Laborism is and how it can work, and we'd like to share it with you.

You'll notice this book reads quite a bit differently than any other economics book. It's not just that it's conversational or that we included actual transcripts of our road-trip conversation in parts; it's something else entirely. So as you read, you'll see that the point of view of the author sometimes changes from *I* (meaning Eric) to *we* (meaning both Eric and Phil). We hope that works and isn't too jarring for you. (See? We just switched to *we* with no warning! You get the idea.)

You'll also find more thoughts in these pages beyond our conversation. Some of what you'll read are those starts and stops I just mentioned. Other passages are clarifications, definitions, or an occasional brief sidetrack to help move the ideas along.

The point of all this is certainly not to bog down an exciting big concept with minutiae. Rather, we hope you'll feel like a participant in a sincere conversation about an idea that we believe can economically *change the world* for millions of people who desperately need change.

Also, as you'll see, we start right out with the big idea—everything you need to know—in the first chapter. But then we anticipate and answer the most common questions or objections someone might have. We think of them as *what abouts*, as in, "What about poor people? What about old people?" We hope organizing our thoughts, some questions, and the answers in such a way makes the read more natural and enjoyable.

Now, what can you expect to learn as you read this book?

We're capitalists who enjoy prosperous lives under capitalism yet believe that capitalism fails far too many people. But rather than just complaining, we wanted to share how we think America can replace capitalism with something better. The benefit will be bringing people out of poverty who want help, leaving people alone who want to be left alone, and dramatically reducing how *America*, the country, is working against *Americans*, the people. That's why we've called this book *America vs. Americans*. We want to show you how America can change, and here's what you can expect to see:

In chapter 1, "Everything We Need," we lay out the basic framework of what American Laborism is and how it will immediately improve the lives of Americans by reversing some damage done by bureaucracy, politics, and capitalism. The point of this chapter is to give you the big idea right up front and hopefully get your mind racing with questions, which we'll answer in the subsequent chapters.

Following that, you might wonder, *Is this the end of America?* Chapter 2 takes a frank look at how changing from capitalism to American Laborism is a reversal of the end of America that we've been on the brink of for decades. Yes, we're changing everything a lot—but not everything we love! Rather, we're trying to help people who need help and stay out of the way of people who don't, so they can prosper, which will get us back to something we can be proud of. We'll break out two sections to discuss "Change Is Coming . . . And It's Needed Fast (But We Better Get It Right)" and "Can the Government Even Help Us in Its Present Form?"

After settling that question, chapter 3, "A Conversation to Change the World for the Better," introduces and boils down Eric and Phil's conversations about the country and the economic system and how it isn't serving Americans well. By sharing our conversation, we aim to make the ideas easy to grasp and put you in the middle of the discussion and the questions you might ask.

In chapter 4, "You Can Think of Laborism as a Tax System If It Helps You," we call out that America's tax system isn't working. We have a much better solution and lay out what to expect and why American Laborism is the only fair option for everyone. We'll also break out a section, "What Does American Laborism Do to Social Security?," because we know how important it is as a part of America's future.

It may be that chapter 5, "Capitalism Failed Because Not Everyone Has Capital," is tough for people to stomach, but the birthplace of capitalism has veered far off course. Beyond just the wealth inequality of America, the opportunities and even the dreams are out of reach for many, and it's because capitalism has worked *too* well. We'll talk about how capitalism got away from us but unfortunately there's nothing better out there. Or at least not yet.

We do feel the need to caution people against the allure of "fixing" capitalism with Marxism. Chapter 6, "Marxism Fails Because Some People Do Have Capital," outlines how any form of Marxism is unworkable for Americans, and we explain why.

Then we get back to what *will* work. Chapter 7, "Why Labor Is

Better—for Everyone—Than Capital," goes into more depth about how American Laborism as a system is inherently fairer to everyone and provides opportunities for people to improve themselves and increase the value of their labor.

Anticipating your questions, we start to answer some in chapter 8, "Who Benefits the Most?" We take a realistic look at the human beings who make up our society, and how a change will impact them in our economic framework. Specifically:

- How can American Laborism help people who can't work?
- Does American Laborism help very poor people?
- What about very old people? How do they fit in?
- Will rich people get anything out of American Laborism?
- What happens to people who work for the federal government?

A big part of American Laborism is explored in chapter 9, "Remaking the Education System." The American education system should be the envy of the world—it's certainly expensive enough to be—but we're going to make it better by giving it to everyone as unlimited, free, and lifelong education. We'll break out sections explaining who will benefit, such as people who have massive student loans, people who want to work for themselves, people who want to advance their education and then get a great job, and even people who want to stay in school forever.

The American military is one aspect of our culture and society that we can be proud of. In chapter 10, "American Laborism and the US Military, Defense Contractors, and Other Companies," we show how under American Laborism, we're going to improve it and pack it full of people who will both spread our ideals and defend our homeland, and we'll discuss those who wish to make a career in the military. We also look at how smaller government affects defense contractors and other businesses, corporations, and even public companies.

Introduction

We tried to stay away from politics, but in chapter 11, "Economics vs. Politics," we're outlining some big changes, including reducing huge sections of our federal government executive branch and all its entrenched departments and programs, and, most importantly, budgets. We will gore a lot of sacred oxen. Topics we'll discuss include:

Will some states want to further restrict their citizens?

Will there be a living wage or UBI?

But socialists and communists aren't willing to let go of control.

Some people aren't wealthy but simply want to punish wealthy people by way of taxation.

An immediate end to tax loopholes.

While American Laborism is a domestic economic system, we do have to address the world we live in and who relies upon American leadership. Chapter 12, "Forever Improving Foreign Affairs," shows how one key to improving America is a complete and total makeover of our foreign affairs policies. This has to happen, and some policies directly impact people living within our borders as well as outside. We'll discuss what happens to foreign aid, how American Laborism affects our immigration policy, and where people who speak other languages fit in.

Most readers might be tempted to immediately turn to chapter 13, "Middle-Class Families, Their Healthcare, and American Laborism," because America needs to take better care of our people. Rather than building a society based on the disgusting class-warfare concept of what the shrinking middle class can bear, we are rebalancing the burden and immediately improving their lives. We'll explain how people with children or families caring for loved ones living with disabilities can benefit. Plus, we'll discuss how to protect middle-class families from job disruptions and our plan for improving American healthcare coverage.

But we're not just dreaming about a better future. In chapter 14, we wonder "How Will Any of This Be Possible?" and the answer is that America is a supercharged dynamo of innovation. We're going to tap into this to immediately improve people's lives. American companies are world-class innovators; the country can integrate blockchain and artificial intelligence, give ourselves a sound currency, and even finally solve the pervasive housing shortages the American government allows America's people to suffer under.

It's a lot to process, we know. We'll end with chapter 15, which is a call to get started, with two specific examples of how "Reducing Government Solves 'America vs. Americans'" and how the steps we've outlined can improve all our lives if we just get started.

Here is how we're changing the world by improving on capitalism. Enjoy!

ERIC and PHIL

CHAPTER 1

EVERYTHING WE NEED

WE HAVE A HEAVY burden with this book. We want to introduce a new economic structure for America. We want it to thoroughly alter how people living in poverty or dissatisfied with their current economic condition receive aid from the federal government. We want to radically reduce our high marginal tax brackets and restructure taxes overall. And we want to realign the foundation of our entire economy from focusing on *capital* to focusing on *labor*.

But we want to do it without handing you a book full of statistics, projections of doom, and the kind of economics discussion that has earned econ the nickname "the dreadful science."

We want this to be a *light read* about *heavy subjects*.

That means the book will present the idea more as a discussion about our beliefs—a conversation of ideas and exploration of thoughts with minimal statistics. If you prefer more history, regulations, and stats, we'll occasionally tell you where to look for them.

But more importantly, we want this book to be a conversation with you. Here's why:

American Laborism is a simple idea. The federal government bureaucracy of the United States of America can provide a safety net of everything everyone who needs a safety net would need, as well as unlimited, free, and lifelong schooling, training, and education.

Yes, from cradle to grave, all needs, and all training or education met for those who need it.

Forever.

But there are a few catches.

First, *everyone* will now pay taxes no matter what their income. But that's not a bad thing! We're going to drastically reduce the tax rates we pay to the federal government. We'll talk more later about the two stages of tax reductions that would come your way in an American Laborism economic system. For now, we'll say that federal taxes for all earners will be no more than 10 percent of all income and capital gains until our federal debt is paid off, and then taxes will drop to no more than 2 percent. In addition to this "earnings" tax, American Laborism will implement a flat 0.25 percent annual "ownership" tax on the entirety of your assets.

This ownership tax will likely be unpopular and compared to the failed wealth taxes Europe experimented with and largely abandoned in the 1990s and 2000s. We believe they failed because people saw relatively little value for the taxes they paid.

You should know that we—both Eric and Phil—do not particularly like implementing a wealth tax. But without it, it's possible that some of the wealthiest companies and people in America would be able to contribute little or nothing in taxes by avoiding income and living off accumulated assets. Our wealth tax—while significantly smaller than those Europe tried—will provide immediately visible American Laborism benefits. Some people might begrudge a 0.25 percent annual wealth tax even though it amounts to only twenty-five dollars out of every ten thousand dollars of wealth you own. It's understandable that people may not like wealth tax, no matter how small. Ordinarily we would be right there with them. But we're proposing it to provide a full safety net and lifetime free education to our fellow citizens, so we won't like it, but we'll pay it.

Second, the entire executive branch of the federal government will be reduced to just three departments:

1. Military
2. Post office
3. Education

But we're not keeping either the Department of Defense or

the Department of Education. We'll replace them with the Military Department and the Advancement Department. The new departments will serve some of the purposes of the ones they're replacing, but they'll also offer other functions as we reduce the size of government.

Unfortunately, with the Department of Defense failing to pass audits mandated by law and the Department of Education leaving America with embarrassing education levels of our students, neither department can continue as is and both need to be replaced by something better.

Regarding education specifically, we wish we didn't have to say this, but the US Department of Education is not currently universally popular. For many Americans, this single department perfectly embodies the "America vs. Americans" concept because the people believe the department guides our education system in an unhealthy direction and refuses to consider the input of its clients: students and parents.

Rest assured, under American Laborism, the new Advancement Department will be thoroughly depoliticized and all ideologies other than providing education will be removed.

Should bias of any kind remain in the department, we will remove the employee or employees promoting it, everyone they hired, and their direct supervisor, and they won't be able to work in the department again for ten years.

We don't care if we need to wind "education" back to the days of little red schoolhouses with a school board representing all of America and one-year term limits for administrators—we aren't handing one-third of our economy to a politicized, biased organization.

And while we're handling the ugly stuff, let us add that every school and workplace participating with American Laborism will have a code of conduct that students, workers, teachers, employers, and administrators will be expected to meet because we are committed to providing education in a safe and respectful manner.

The code of conduct will, at the very least, mirror the laws of the locality the school, residences, and workplace are located in. There will be no tolerance for violence, controlled substances, harassment, or discrimination. Anyone who violates the code of conduct will be suspended or expelled and lose all access to benefits.

With that said, let's get back to the three proposed departments as a whole.

Literally, any service or program that the federal government executive branch participates in will be conducted by one, two, or three of these branches—Military Department, Post Office, and/or Advancement Department. Yes, intelligence, scientific programs, endowments for arts, even space exploration will either be conducted by these departments or it won't be part of the federal government executive branch bureaucracy. Plus, they'll have to live with a balanced federal budget, meaning no more deficit spending.

We'll briefly touch on what happens to the existing departments later in the book, but an example would be to reassign the Department of Justice to the US Senate with judicial branch oversight. The Department of the Interior can be folded into the United States Post Office and immediately reduced in size and scope. Those are just two examples, but they give you the idea.

Therefore, the entire federal government "safety net" system of the United States up until now—everything from unemployment to SNAP or WIC or disability or scholarships or grants for anyone needing any assistance from the federal government—will be the responsibility of these three departments.

Yes, everyone who needs anything from the safety net of the federal government will still get what they need. For the rest of their life, if they need it. If you need shelter, that is what you will receive. Food? Same. Schooling, training, or education? Unlimited and lifelong. But understand that by *education*, we don't mean just college. Education takes many forms, from learning English to advanced degrees, trades, certifications . . . anything that can make your labor more valuable.

But there's a catch: it won't be in cash, check, ACH, credits, debits, cards, vouchers, digital currency, or any kind of money.

We can do this because everyone who receives any assistance and education will also be required to pitch in by doing jobs that benefit the community (at least one full day of work per week) and attend at least one full, eight-hour day of class each week. That can be broken up into two-hour blocks on four days or four-hour blocks on two days.

These are the minimum requirements to get benefits. You always have the option of taking more classes than the minimum or providing more than the minimum amount of labor. If you take more classes, they're free. If you work extra, you get paid for the extra part.

Therefore, people will also enjoy the privilege and obligation of advancing their training or education if they want benefits from the federal government.

If someone needs benefits but doesn't want to continue their education, they also have the option to enroll in the military or work for the US Post Office. Simply put, if you just want federal benefits and don't want to work full time, you go to school and work one day a week.

One goal of American Laborism is to get anyone who needs help educated to a point where they don't.

To be clear, neither the United States military nor post office will be part of the safety net. They will maintain suitable requirements to be part of their organization, just as they do today. Perhaps they can even become more selective with who they accept. They will be significant parts of the future federal government, but only the Advancement Department is tasked with helping anyone who might need help. The Post Office will be tasked with delivering mail and certain other agency and department responsibilities that it will absorb, and the military will be tasked with maintaining the world's most effective fighting force. Now, because our military is as skilled at building and managing as they are at breaking things, we may ask for them to assist in peaceful activities such as building houses or schools or absorbing other departments and agencies and sharing oversight with the Advancement Department and United States Postal Service (USPS) as appropriate.

Anyone who doesn't need any assistance or safety net from the federal government will have the privilege of paying far lower taxes and can pursue any education, employment, entrepreneurship, or lack of any of these that they wish.

And there's one last benefit American Laborism provides to our society and our fellow Americans: Because Laborism takes care of the needs of everyone when they need help, and those people are increasing their education and contributing back to our society simultaneously, we as a nation can be proud that we can provide for literally everyone here in a dignified, respectable manner.

American Laborism literally provides the needs and unlimited education for anyone who wishes for it, while reducing the burden of paying for it from our most fortunate brothers and sisters by reducing their taxes (while making sure they pay what they owe).

We're going to need a stable, asset-backed dollar to make this happen. That's not impossible, and we'll talk about how we can do that, thanks to blockchain.

We know . . . it sounds like magical economic pixie-dust dreaming. It's not. It is fairness, educational advancement, and personal responsibility.

CHAPTER 2

IS THIS THE END OF AMERICA?

YOU MAY HAVE READ the previous chapter and are asking, "So . . . is this the end of America?"

No, it isn't the end of America—although the changes we are proposing are indeed significant.

Replace capitalism. End progressive taxes. Shrink the federal government. Provide free lifetime education. We can see why someone might think the America they know is ending. But you could also argue that we're getting closer to the beginning of America—and doing so in a way that is fair and respectful to all Americans.

For the next few minutes—however long it takes to read this chapter—we want you to imagine yourself on a long, pleasant road trip to a destination you're excited to get to, much like the long drive Phil and I had ahead of us when we started talking about American Laborism not long ago.

Also, pretend you are with an acquaintance, and you are having a conversation to pass the time. Imagine that the question of where we are today in terms of how well America takes care of Americans comes up. Maybe even the concept of America working *against* Americans—America vs. Americans—is mentioned.

If you don't think you both will agree on the topic, you might be concerned that the discussion could become heated. Alternatively, you might feel as though it would be best to keep your thoughts to yourself, in order to avoid any disagreements that might taint the rest of the trip with negativity.

Paradoxically, virtually everyone can think of ways that America is on the brink of failing our fellow Americans, be it social issues, wealth inequality, runaway taxation, outrageous debt, or crime. Yet because each of us sees differently how America is failing us, it is likely that talking about it will be challenging.

For many people, this could be a difficult situation, but it doesn't have to be . . . if you go purple. By that, we mean try to find some common ground by approaching the conversation from the standpoint that, even if you don't know how another person feels about America right now, there must be something you both agree on. The benefit of doing that—finding common ground—is that together we can help people who need help, stay out of the way of people who don't so they can prosper, and work on building an America we can all be proud of.

Take a minute to read through the following quotes. As you're reading, think about the meaning behind what the speaker is saying. You'll likely see some that you immediately agree with—and some you don't. Spend an extra second on the quotes that you don't agree with, and allow yourself to think, *I wish that could be true.*

"We are all one family in the world. Building a community that empowers everyone to attain their full potential through respecting each other's dignity, rights, and responsibilities makes the world a better place to live." (attributed to St. John Paul II, "Solidarity and Mutuality," Center for Mission)

"Government is not the solution to our problem; government is the problem." (President Ronald Reagan, Inaugural Address, January 20, 1981, Ronald Reagan Presidential Foundation & Institute)

"The test of our progress is not whether we add more to the abundance of those who have much; it is whether we provide enough for those who have too little." (President Franklin D. Roosevelt, Second Inaugural Address, January 20, 1937, Yale Law School, Lillian Goldman Law Library)

"For the economy to grow, government must get out of the way." (Senator Rand Paul, Conservative Political Action Conference [CPAC] on March 14, 2013, in Washington, DC)

"Education is not the filling of a pail, but the lighting of a fire." (Often attributed to William Butler Yeats)

"The true test of a civilization is not the census, nor the size of the cities, nor the crops, but the kind of man that the country produces." (Ralph Waldo Emerson, *Society and Solitude,* 1870)

"Together, we can and must create an economy and government that works for all Americans and not just the 1 percent." (Senator Bernie Sanders, Fox News op-ed April 14, 2019)

"Government doesn't have to be the enemy, but too much government has produced a new kind of inequality in America: opportunity inequality." (Senator Marco Rubio, *American Dreams: Restoring Economic Opportunity for Everyone,* 2015)

"I believe that a child going without an education is a crime." (Vice President Kamala Harris, *Huffington Post,* March 18, 2010, when she was San Francisco DA)

"Education is the closest thing to magic." (Senator Tim Scott, "Sen. Tim Scott: Education Is the Closest Thing to Magic," episode 2, Independent Women's Forum, February 7, 2023)

Obviously, being able to see value in other people's thoughts and opinions so you can get along with them is not just a good idea for a car ride, but for life in general. It's an integral part of being an American that we're out of practice doing—which is disheartening because we all want to be part of the same thing.

And that same thing is the American dream—the belief that anyone, regardless of their background, can achieve success and prosperity through hard work and determination. This is what gives people hope and drives them to achieve their goals. The idea of the American dream has been a central part of American culture for decades. As Americans, we are constantly working toward similar ideals and a way of life that includes:

1. **Education.** America is known for having some of the most prestigious universities in the world, and many people believe that getting a good education is critical for success. Everyone should have the opportunity to empower themselves and improve their lives through education. Many people come to America for the opportunity to receive an education, which they know will improve their lives in the long run.

2. **Entrepreneurship.** In America, entrepreneurship and innovation have always been highly valued. Our country has a long and rich heritage of inventive thinking, which has allowed us to develop countless enterprises that reach well beyond our borders. The country has a supportive environment for business startups, with many successful companies being born as a result.

3. **Free Speech.** The First Amendment to the US Constitution protects the right to free speech, meaning that people can express their opinions without interference or punishment from the government. The First Amendment guarantees the freedom of speech and expression, which is a core value of American society.

4. **Cultural Diversity.** The United States is a country with a rich

tapestry of cultures and traditions, and its diversity is one of its most valuable assets. The country is home to people from all over the world, and this mix of cultures has created a unique American identity that can be seen in various aspects of American culture.

5. **Democracy.** This word seems to change definitions constantly, but America is a *democratic republic*, which means its citizens can choose their leaders by voting them into elected positions. A true democratic system inspires not only those within the country but also those around the world by providing political freedom and the ability of people to shape their own future.

The role of government in society and how much power it should have are hotly debated topics in America. Liberals and conservatives have very different views on these issues, and their beliefs have shaped the political landscape of the country.

Liberals often believe government has a duty to provide for the common good of society and ensure that all citizens have access to basic necessities such as healthcare, education, and housing. They believe a powerful government can help create a more just and equal society, and that it is government's responsibility to safeguard vulnerable groups of people and ensure that everyone has an equal opportunity to prosper.

Conservatives, on the other hand, believe government's role should be limited and that individuals should have more freedom to make their own decisions. They argue that a strong government can have a negative impact on personal liberty and economic growth, and that it is the responsibility of individuals to take care of themselves and their families.

Can anyone say right now that either "side"—and we call that out with quotes, because we are different "sides" as much as the left hand is separated from the right hand (separate but still connected as two parts of one body)—is getting what they want?

This is why it's critical to depoliticize the Department of Education, shut it down, and start fresh with the Advancement Department. To achieve the promise of the American dream, we need to come together as a country and accept some change. We need to build a movement that everyone can agree on.

Purple thinking is knowing this is possible and giving everyone what is best for them at an acceptable cost. American Laborism isn't a compromise. It is no less of a balanced solution that includes everyone than purple thinking is, which requires equal parts of red and blue.

Change Is Coming . . . and It's Needed Fast (But We Better Get It Right)

There are many reasons we believe that purple thinking will benefit America.

The most obvious reason is that America suffers from division among our people. It's evident everywhere that, as a country of people who agree on the basic American dream principles we laid out, we seem to be looking for things to disagree on. We won't go into politics here, and truth be told, some of the things Americans disagree on are important to their respective sides, and they don't *want* to agree. But this is an economic improvement we're undertaking with American Laborism. While we'll acknowledge that we're divided, we're going to focus on the part that we can turn into a purple agreement of how best to provide a lifetime of free education and an improved safety net for people who need it.

So a benefit that purple thinking can provide is at least we can agree that the Americans who need help can be helped by the safety net we're providing . . . and that currently, America is spending trillions of dollars, but Americans' problems aren't being solved.

Another purple benefit is simply receiving the dividends of that unlimited, free education. Who could argue that our society wouldn't be improved by anyone who wants to become better educated having access to free training and advancement?

But there are also some powerful examples of why it's critical that we get this right—and fast. Let's dive into how a tool we plan to use to improve the delivery of customized education—artificial intelligence (AI)—is so powerful that it could serve as a disruption simultaneously. Worse, if AI does disrupt our economy or labor force, and we haven't "gone purple" with American Laborism, our government and our present benefit programs are in no way prepared to handle it.

To offer some background, AI has the potential to disrupt our economy by making some jobs easier, some unnecessary, and others so hyperefficient that employers and employees will have a lot of adjusting to do. We don't even know all the ramifications and changes that AI will bring, because AI is rapidly developing.

Some AI technologies can replace graphic artists and photographers by creating artwork or photorealistic images that may have previously required models, illustrators, photographers, lighting and makeup pros, and whole crews of talented artists to create.

Other AI technologies can read, understand, and summarize huge amounts of information that formerly required trained professionals such as lawyers, business administrators, engineers, doctors, and subject experts to accomplish. More than that, AI can do this work in minutes, replacing untold hours of human effort.

Other AI technologies can create pleasing visual or audio artworks, such as movies and songs that previously might have required a movie studio and hundreds of people and months to make. (This is exactly why the Writers Guild of America and the Screen Actors Guild went on strike in 2023.) Or imagine a recording studio with highly trained professionals all being replaced by a hardworking computer that may create a movie or song without hiring a soul.

Other AI technologies can look for (and find) patterns in data that could allow anything from medical or scientific research to criminal investigations to become lightning fast.

One thing is certain, though: AI will be able to build custom lesson plans and educational curriculum for people seeking to learn. If a core offering of American Laborism is access to training and education for all people, it makes sense that AI can be used to determine what a student knows, what they want to study, what their education goals are, and the best path to achieve that. Once AI starts helping our students, it can also determine what improvements or changes need to be made to the lessons to best suit each individual.

Imagine having schooling custom-built for you, rather than having to learn the same as everyone else assigned from a specific textbook. The possibilities of how AI can help us are just as exciting as the threats it poses to job security are scary.

In fact, years before the AI we know today was even possible, the Massachusetts Institute of Technology (MIT) conducted a review of what it thought the disruptive effects of AI might be.[1]

The report found that, contrary to most people's fears—which are that robots, automation, and AI would render blue-collar workers jobless—most of the expected disruption MIT found would instead occur among *white*-collar professionals.

The report revealed a lot, but there are two important findings we want to discuss. First, MIT pointed to another prediction that AI will create as many jobs as it destroys, and that could be as much as 47 percent of jobs. (Yes, it used that scary word—*destroys*!) If you still don't understand what disruption means when a new technology enters the job arena, this could be the definition of disruption. Destroying nearly half (47 percent) of all jobs and replacing them with different jobs—that is a near-perfect picture of disruption. Wherever you work, imagine half of the workforce gone and replaced by people doing something completely different.

The second finding almost proves the case for American Laborism all by itself. AI disruption is expected to affect white-collar workers the most, "they may find it easier to retrain or find alternate roles"[2] —which is exactly a benefit of free, unlimited, lifelong education.

We believe there will certainly be disruption; some people will lose jobs and need to seek other jobs that may require further education or retraining (which American Laborism will happily provide). However, the leaps in efficiency that AI makes possible in some areas will increase our economy and—ironically—drive a need for more labor. Yes, we think the job-disrupting technology will drive *more* jobs thanks to efficiencies and processes that took days and weeks that will be reduced to just minutes.

That leads us to the conclusion of the labor disruption possibility. And for that we decided to ask an AI large language model to help us write . . . about itself. Here's what we got:

Increasing labor can play a crucial role in managing the disruption caused by AI (Artificial Intelligence). As automation and AI technologies advance, there is legitimate concern about potential job displacement.

However, by actively investing in labor-intensive sectors, such as healthcare, education, creative industries, and sustainable infrastructure, we can create new avenues for employment and ensure a smooth transition. These sectors rely on uniquely human skills, such as empathy, creativity, critical thinking, and problem-solving, which are difficult to replicate with AI. By expanding opportunities in these areas, we can harness the potential of human labor to complement AI technologies, fostering a collaborative and synergistic relationship that benefits both productivity and society as a whole.

Additionally, focusing on reskilling and upskilling programs can empower individuals to adapt to the changing demands of the job market and equip them with the skills necessary to thrive alongside AI. Ultimately, embracing an inclusive and proactive approach to labor can help mitigate the disruption caused by AI and create a future where humans and machines work harmoniously.

All that sounds great . . . certainly it's a positive spin.

But there are two sides of the coin, and we believe our current government systems are in no way prepared for managing the disruption we'll see while we walk on the path from firing to reskilling to rehiring to "working together harmoniously."

It's not outrageous to imagine that plans to spend trillions of dollars in the name of helping us deal with AI are already being drawn up by our government, which seems to want to spend trillions of dollars every chance it gets.

Since this is an economics book, we can say (without being political) that we believe our government has used the strategy of spending trillions of dollars to solve a temporary problem so many times that the purchasing power of the world's most powerful currency—the US dollar—has suffered as a result. Most people aren't aware of the fact that we've lost 15 percent[3] of the value of our dollars just since the beginning of the COVID-19 pandemic!

The pandemic was of course a tragedy that resulted in a damaged economy and a heartbreaking loss of life. Hopefully, we'll never see another event like that in America's future. But the coming AI disruption is different from a pandemic, and there's no possibility that we won't see AI disruption. (And after that, we may see another technological disruption wave based on quantum computers. We'll save worrying about that for when the threat is closer, as it's likely years away. The good news is that our government is attempting to prepare for it. The bad news is nobody knows what kind of threats quantum computer attacks will be, so preparing for them is extremely challenging.)

Can the Government Even Help Us in Its Present Form?

We also have to admit that the way our federal government is doing things in America could be improved. At least we can agree that numbers show our safety net programs are performing poorly, cost too much, and are often subjected to extremely costly fraud.

Consider this: America's programs, expenditures, debt, and deficit spending are threatening America. In addition, we do not believe all our laws and government practices are in our ultimate best interest. One example would be increasing military spending (which we aren't against) while the US Department of Defense continually fails to account for trillions of dollars of the money it receives (which is illegal and should be unacceptable). Or how about our Internal Revenue Service scrutinizing citizens who use online services for transactions under $1,000 but ignoring people who fail to pay millions in back taxes? How can anyone think our government's America vs. Americans activities are sustainable? In fact, reducing the size and scope of government and shifting our benefits into a generous but in-kind style is what will prevent the end of America!

Here's one example of improper handling: the cash benefits we pay—by literally taking taxpayer money or borrowing money—are often stolen by fraudsters. That means Americans literally subsidize fraud and theft, much of which is taking advantage of American programs meant to support the needy.

This is another symptom of a government that is too big and too removed from the constituents: when billions of dollars are stolen from taxpayers who have no way of stopping it, because it's done by way of programs their very government set up and maintains.

Blake Hall, the founder and CEO of ID.me, an

identity-verification technology company that often partners with state governments and federal agencies, tracks this fraud. Whether you are red or blue, there's no benefit to Americans that hundreds of billions of our dollars meant to help one another have been stolen from us. Even though we are divided on many issues as a country, that is one thing we can all agree on.

The following are some examples of America's overly generous cash benefits being stolen or fraudulently acquired by people who don't deserve them. We're sharing this because every dollar that goes to a thief or a fraudster is a dollar—plus the costs of *administering* that dollar—that could have gone to help a needy American.

A 2022 report by the Office of the Inspector General indicates $400 billion likely went to improper or fraudulent unemployment claims in 2020 and 2021.[4] This was, of course, when the world was scrambling to deal with the economic fallout of shutting our economy due to the outbreak of COVID-19. Nevertheless, NPR reported that Michigan alone paid out $8.5 billion in fraudulent jobless claims during the pandemic.[5] There are at least forty-nine other states in which the benefits meant for citizens ended up in criminals' hands.

Hall says it's possible that many of these fraudulent benefits were likely paid to criminals in foreign countries based on known hacks and espionage that the US Department of Justice uncovered.[6] That means it is highly likely that a large sum of money was stolen from the support programs in place for the American people and given to foreign criminals, simply because our benefits system is easy to exploit.

Clearly, this needs to be improved. If you ask the question, "Is American Laborism the end of America?," perhaps the answer might be that it's the end of America being robbed blind because our generosity hasn't kept up with criminals' ability to steal from us.

You see, if the safety net benefits are in-kind and delivered personally, there's no way to steal them. Moreover, reports indicate that much of the benefits-theft occurred electronically. That makes sense. Sophisticated thieves have applied for multiple benefits, and the electronic money systems we use simply sent out the money.

And it isn't just sophisticated thieves that our present system can't keep up with. A report from the Department of Labor indicates some thieves were so brazen that they filed unemployment insurance cases with the same Social Security numbers in multiple states.[7]

You cannot do any of this with in-kind benefits. That means theft stops immediately, and the folks who deserve the benefits get 100 percent of them.

Much of these findings have been presented in an analysis by Reason.com, in which they lay out proof in an easy-to-digest way that $400 billion earmarked for benefits for the American people during the COVID-19 pandemic response were stolen.[8]

But before you discount this problem as merely a well-intentioned, overly generous COVID-19 response flush with so much cash that it was temporarily impossible to track and properly administer every dollar, you should know that a 2019 YouGov survey *before* the pandemic found that around half of Americans were distrustful of our benefits programs.[9]

But something else is revealed in the survey, which states:

> Most Americans believe the government provides "too much" public assistance to the rich (59%) and "not enough" to the middle class (53%) or the poor (51%). But, while most Americans say the lower economic classes are not given enough support through government programs, there is not overwhelming support for increased funding to those organizations.[10]

That impossible paradox—not enough support given, yet no overwhelming support for increased funding—is solved by the

American Laborism safety net in-kind benefits program.

So let's get back to the question, which might be expanded to read: If American Laborism drastically reduces government, lowers taxes, and shifts our so-generous-they-can-be-easily-robbed benefits . . . is this the end of America as we know it?

The answer is (still) absolutely not. Though it might be the end of overspending on programs that leave hundreds of thousands of people—perhaps millions of people—without sufficient support while excessively taxing everyone. It would be more accurate to say that this is the beginning of an America where we can be proud of ourselves for taking better care of people, reducing waste, and thinking of an improved future where anyone who wants to can increase the value of their labor with a lifelong free education.

That is something both "sides" of America can agree on.

We need this better system before the worst of the AI disruption overwhelms our current programs—let alone any future pandemics or quantum computing disruptions.

The role of government in society is a complex and deeply divided issue that people have been debating for centuries. Liberals and conservatives have such contrasting perspectives on this subject, and their ideologies have influenced the political discussion in America for many years. While both sides have valid arguments, it is ultimately up to the American people to decide what kind of society they want to create and what role they want their government to play in shaping that society.

Government Should Be a Reflection of the People's Will and Not the Other Way Around

American Laborism is a system in which we all get what we want and put a stop to the government of America working against delivering the needs of Americans.

American Laborism is not the end of America; it's the end of

America vs. Americans.

Another question you might have is, what do we mean by "Capitalism has failed a capitalist nation"?

It is certainly true that capitalism has lifted more people out of poverty than any other economic system in history. In America, there is a greater number of people making more money than there has been at any point in the past. People own homes. They're starting businesses. The entire country's measure of capitalism working— GDP, or what we produce as a country—is high and, setting aside COVID, virtually always increasing.

Our standard of living as a country is high, and our median income as individuals is higher than most other countries.

So how is that failure?

The answer: our GDP, currently $23 trillion, is indeed the highest in the world. And our *per capita* numbers also rank highly. But our government is spending more than it's taking in. The cumulative US budget deficit for the 2024–2033 period is projected to total $20.2 trillion, or 6.1 percent of GDP.

That's about $2 trillion a year on a budget that is only around $4 trillion a year. So we either need to cut government spending in half to balance the budget, increase taxes by another $2 trillion a year, or keep printing money to pay for things we can't afford.

Under capitalism and common-sense accounting, if you are continuously going deeper into debt and never paying any of it off, you've failed and will eventually go bankrupt because it is not financially viable. There's no alternative.

But here's the sad part. The $4 trillion we are spending isn't guaranteeing that our citizens live at an acceptable standard, and our government is so poorly managed that even with another $2 trillion a year to cover the deficit, there would be no guarantee we'd meet any kind of standard to take care of people who need it. Even though GDP may have increased, homelessness, poverty, and food insecurity have also risen. Furthermore, we can't sufficiently educate people; we are declining in education compared to the rest of the world.

So it seems that capitalism has not failed those who are wealthy, but it is not providing enough care or assistance for everyone else, and we are going into debt as a result.

That's a failure both liberals and conservatives, left and right, and anyone on a long road trip who's brave enough to discuss politics can agree on.

CHAPTER 3

A CONVERSATION TO CHANGE THE WORLD FOR THE BETTER

[AUTHORS' NOTE: We're including some of the conversation between Eric and Phil that we mentioned previously. We want you to experience the introduction to American Laborism just as Phil was introduced to it and read along with the questions he had. As you'll see, there are times when Eric does most of the talking—because Phil is trying to ask questions that get the ideas out! Some of our conversation will include ideas you'll see explored further in the book. At the risk of being only slightly repetitive, we wanted to keep the conversational flow as close as possible to the first time we discussed American Laborism. Plus, since this represents the first time Phil heard about it, you'll see that he probably asks some of the same questions you're already wondering.]

Eric

I'd like to introduce to the world what I believe is an improvement on both capitalism and communism or Marxism. You don't need to have a perfect understanding of either to know there are plenty of examples of capitalism that have resulted in unsatisfactory results for some people living in capitalist societies. Conversely, others are thrilled with capitalism and the opportunities it provides.

Until recently, I would count myself in that camp. Capitalism certainly has a lot to offer, and I've done well under capitalism.

Likewise, there are numerous examples of Marxist, socialist, and communist societies where some people do well and others are left behind. Some people don't like these systems because they don't feel they are fair. Other people focus on the ideals of Marxist societies while refusing to address how damaging they are to those who don't want to live under them.

Just by knowing and understanding this dichotomy—that there are two types of dominant governance people inflict on one another in terms of economic governance—is important. I'm not talking about the difference between democracy or autocracy or anarchy or anything else like that. I'm talking more about what kind of economic system we are stuck with.

Those two are the dominant ones that are not working, and I think I have a solution for the world. And it isn't just to mix the two together!

We've tried both of those, and both have their positive possibilities, and both have their weaknesses. I also don't want to make anybody think I'm not patriotic or don't believe America doesn't have the best to offer.

Phil

I don't think wanting to improve America is coming off as being unpatriotic. We are long due for an overhaul, and the system could be much more efficient.

Eric

Exactly, America could be done better. And we've got many people living in poverty or even homeless. And I also don't believe the entire society should be changed, held back, or punished in any way to make up for the people who need the most help.

I sometimes feel like communism, with the famous line, "From those according to their ability to those according to their need," could be a great operating system for anything but *human beings.*

It's an interesting idea that might work well on a computer network or with robots, which might be programmed to identify weaknesses and then provide assistance. But to apply it to humans, especially Americans, you would need to remove ego and desire— and frankly, any number of human traits—for a system like communism or Marxism to work.

Maybe the most important trait that prevents communism from working for humans is our innate ability to game a system.

Phil
Humans can find a way to game any system . . . any system at all. And when people's lives are at stake, that is not what you would want.

Eric
True. I think that what we've seen throughout history is that in a capitalist society, the people who have the most money end up separating themselves from the rest of the population, and in a communist society, there is also a similar separation between the upper and lower classes. And I have a better idea if we take the best that both of those have to offer.

Phil
You're saying there doesn't have to be two extremes, right?

Eric
Right.

Phil
But there isn't any kind of middle ground that they can both meet on. They're too different. There's no way to fairly add free market to Marxism without the people at the top getting everything and the people at the bottom staying at the bottom.

Eric

That's why we need to create the middle ground. And by the way, I don't know how much you know about socialism, but that's not it. In no way, shape, or form is socialism a middle ground between the devastation of the human spirit that communism offers and the extreme wealth inequality of capitalism. Rather than taking the best of both systems, socialism takes the worst. You end up with communism's despair and capitalism's caste system.

So instead, let's talk about finding a new way that takes the best of capitalism, but also ensures everyone at the so-called bottom is taken care of. We can game out every weakness or argument, or every "What about this?" that someone could come up with, and solve it.

Phil

Now, when you start tweaking the economy, it will also have carried over into other facets of life, right?

Eric

Absolutely. Even though this isn't about voting or democracy, I'm about to say something that is such a huge departure from our current economic state that it would require many voting changes, and systems that we're used to would have to change. And that's just the beginning.

Phil

It's an overhaul.

Eric

Yeah. This beginning preamble is just a way to let people who enjoy the capitalist system know there'll be more to enjoy about this, and for those who still believe the fairy tale of any kind of communist or . . .

Phil

Socialist.

Eric

. . . socialist system (and I use those words lightly), you'll find things you like about this. A lot of this has to do with the fact that I think the American dream has gradually become disconnected from American policy.

If this were a book, I would call it America vs. Americans. *The laws and rules of America are working against most of us. What you think you have as an American and what you think you gain from the American system are not what the Founders intended when they established this country.*

And I get it. It's a different country, right? We all have fast cars and property rights that are different from when America was first born. In addition, there have been many improvements to the American system over the years, such as voting rights being extended to groups of people who were not originally included when the Constitution was written. This also includes freedoms and equalities that weren't even thought of at the time.

We have trade with places around the globe that's entirely different from centuries ago. We've morphed into a society of consumers who buy goods without giving any thought to keeping people working and prospering in our own communities. That's just how we live now.

We also have to think about how politics, rules, and laws have changed. Yes, we have improved America. In the process of making our society better, we have also created a rule book, our legal code, that is so complex and confusing that an average person would need to dedicate their life to it to understand it.

I think that in order for the federal government to be more effective, we need to get back to the basics and ensure that it can address every citizen's needs. Much of what you may want as optional should be shifted from the federal government's responsibilities to states or municipalities. What I'm trying to say is that the federal government should provide a safety net for everyone and then let states and cities offer additional programs as they see fit.

Phil

So what we need to do is prevent the federal government from having too much control. Sounds like returning power and responsibilities to the states in some capacity.

Eric

Not a pure federalist type of capacity, but more in line with those who want to limit the federal government, reduce taxes, and change the services offered by the federal government to a point where it can balance a budget and pay off our debts.

Maybe we should shift more personalized services to states and municipalities. And the benefits we'll get from that are— and this will sound fantastical—lower taxes, balanced budgets, reduced fraud, and laws that can easily be enforced. Everybody gets their needs met, and people who want to exceed their needs, such as capitalists or people who want to achieve more, earn more, and own more, can do all that without restriction.

I believe that if we implement this system, one benefit will be to solve the two-victim current system with our national border.

Phil

What do you mean by two-victim? *Who are the two victims?*

Eric

People who cross the border without documentation are one victim, and America is the other. We can go deeper about this later, but I feel that undocumented people are victims of our system. They often have to pay very high prices to get here, work for lower wages, live in fear, and sometimes don't have access to everything they would like if they had the proper documentation. It's not always living the best life they could.

Phil

So, can you explain a little about how America is a victim?

Eric

One of the issues with undocumented people is that we don't always know who they are or where they come from. We can't entirely integrate them into our society. We can't treat them as equal, productive members of the community. And the fact that there may be tens of millions of undocumented people here, with millions coming and going each year, means anyone who wants to do America harm can get lost in the crowd. It is unfortunate that drug cartels and people-smugglers are such prevalent criminal activities, as it makes it difficult to give legitimate migrants the treatment they deserve.

Implementing American Laborism allows us to welcome all immigrants who want a better life; that basic desire is not something anybody would hold against them. And this system can grow to include everybody. And whether it grows beyond the borders of America, we can share the American Laborism framework with the rest of the world. I think they'll see something they like.

Phil

There are probably a million questions that we need to return to.

Eric

So, ask a ton of questions!

But the most general, basic idea of American Laborism is that we tried capitalism. The truth is that capitalism, while it may have worked well in the beginning, has not been as successful over time. Once someone amasses an absolutely system-altering amount of capital—and this happens in capitalist, socialist, and communist societies—they can push everyone around, right?

People with capital can push laws around or skirt them. I'm by no means implying that people with billions of dollars got it through any illegal fashion. But that level of wealth makes it difficult for a society that sees both billionaires and those in poverty to think it's a fair society, so we're going to solve that.

We're going to be a fair society . . . thanks to American Laborism.

And with Laborism, I don't mean the labor movement, and I don't mean labor unions. This brand of Laborism means that we all own our labor, and we should respect that. Labor should be the base unit that we can all offer to one another, communicate with to one another, and value among one another, right?

If I want to provide my labor for a cost, or someone wants to hire my labor, or I want to withhold my labor, that's entirely my decision and no one else's. And under Laborism, everyone's labor will be valuable, and they can raise that value when they educate themselves. That's why education is a core part of American Laborism.

Phil

Define labor.

Eric

Most people immediately understand it as simply work *or*

working. *Let's expand that, though. Labor is a productive activity that you engage in for which you receive something in return.*

Phil
So the "something" is not just money or wages but also value.

Eric
Right. Maybe I'm in the trades, and I'm using my skills, time, knowledge, and education to provide quality workmanship that is beneficial to others. Or maybe I'm a skilled person who uses my brain and applies it toward my labor, such as a doctor, an attorney, an accountant, or an engineer. Or maybe I'm a physical laborer whose skills may still be developing, so it's my time that I can offer as valuable.

Phil
This whole system is based on labor. Let's talk through this. The term labor *can be a bit vague and have different meanings depending on the context. Basically, it's all about the effort we put into producing goods and services in a functional economy. You know, people work for businesses and get paid for their work, which they then use to buy stuff they need.*

Now, businesses can use this labor to create their own products and services that people want to buy. And when we talk about labor, we can think of it in different ways—such as the mental, physical, and social aspects of it.

But here's the thing: labor is just one of the four essential components for production in an economy. The other three are capital, natural resources, and entrepreneurship. Together, they all help create the supply, and then consumers like us create the demand.

So Laborism contends that if there are four essential

components of production, and labor and capital are two, Laborism favors labor—which is plentiful, and maybe fairer—in the way capitalism focuses on capital, which gets really focused on a small number of capitalists who actually have the capital.

Eric

We're improving capitalism by recognizing the higher value of labor.

But American Laborism will respect all four elements—capital, natural resources, entrepreneurship, but especially labor—and give everybody an opportunity to better themselves.

The part I expect to be a stumbling block when implementing this is that we will initiate American Laborism and respect labor by reducing the role of the federal government to only three parts of our society.

Phil

Reducing the role of the government is critical to American Laborism, but do you expect there will be people who don't want to reduce the size of the government?

Eric

I do. But the plan isn't to keep everything the same and just have a smaller version of it. I wouldn't want that, either. The plan is to reduce the government by eliminating a lot of departments and keeping—maybe even expanding—just three parts. The federal government would maintain our armed forces and our postal system, and we would offer unlimited, free education at the federal level. Those are the only three executive branch roles of the federal government under an American Laborism system.

Notice I'm not talking about the judicial branch. Obviously, we will still have laws, so criminals will be taken care of.

If you have a need, if you are hungry, if you are undereducated, if you have children and can't entirely take care of them yourself while you work or go to school, or you have other basic human needs, the federal government will provide that either through the military, education, or postal service. That means those three departments must step up and be ready to solve the problems of anyone who needs help on a federal basis.

Now, obviously, states and municipalities, churches and other religious institutions, and so on can implement their own levels of help. But on a federal level, we're going to look at every citizen as equal and as the same. There will be absolutely no discrimination among citizens whatsoever on a federal basis. In fact, we could probably extend this to all humans; it doesn't even matter with American Laborism that you're American. Whether you're a citizen or not, we'll provide these services to literally any human who needs them and has a documented right to receive them, such as refugees and documented immigrants.

So we would have a Military Department, an Advancement Department, and a Post Office. Obviously, before anything else, you have to establish some ground rules and expectations. First of all, none of these three departments will simply hand out cash to people who come with genuine needs.

There is no federal unemployment cash program. There are no food stamps. There's no welfare. There's nothing like that anymore. We're not solving problems with capital, with cash. We can solve them with labor, and we can ensure that people are taken care of, but not by paying them. And we're going to implement a system that if you need something and come to the federal government to solve it, most likely your need will be solved by someone else who also had a need.

Phil

At the foundation of this, what's going on is if someone has a need, they don't just turn to the government and get some money. Instead, the government they turn to is offering support if they're willing to pursue more education. And what the government provides—since the government is us—*is organizing the people who have needs to help other people who have needs.*

I'm picturing someone who maybe has a job but isn't earning enough to make ends meet. Since there's no more cash benefits, I'm thinking of it being as simple as whatever your skill or talent is— provide your skilled labor for six or seven other people, and they'll do the same. So now I can see how you'd say this could scale up to as many people as would need it. If there aren't cash benefits, theoretically everyone can be part of this.

But that brings me to my next question: paying for everyone's unlimited education. Who's actually paying? Billionaires?

Eric

Unfortunately, this is something we've been hoodwinked on. Sadly, we've been told that the wealthiest among us, the billionaires, have enough money to pay for whatever we need. And these are typically vote-gathering schemes of whatever new program a politician pitches. Now, I agree with providing free education, and I believe our system can provide that free education, but not by raising taxes.

Phil

How, then? Free isn't really free. It has a cost.

Eric

Because everybody's pitching in, a little tax revenue will go a long way.

Phil

Will what kind of labor people provide be clearly defined? Sure, everyone may have valuable labor to provide. But is it necessarily a skill required by the federal government, and more importantly, who decides? For example, if you are wiping down tables in exchange for food, who are the participants? Is the federal government providing food? Is the restaurant government-owned? Is the restaurant getting free labor? Does the restaurant partner with the federal government? Would there be incentives to participate? Could there be potential for corruption, with privately owned companies doing "favors" in exchange for partnerships with the federal government?

Eric

Those are great questions, but you're going somewhat sideways. Don't think in terms of a restaurant; think in terms of working as part of the school. Of course, people can still work elsewhere, wherever they want . . . and they will want to, because if they want compensation, they have to go find it somewhere else. That should satisfy capitalists and people who are used to buying labor.

Phil

Where are you finding it?

Eric

The private labor market, or people wanting and getting jobs, or companies wanting and needing workers . . . that isn't going to change at all. Anyone can do their own thing or work anywhere for anyone they want. It's only if you want benefits that you sign up for free school and contribute one day of labor . . . but that isn't compensated other than getting you into school and benefits.

Phil

Unless your job is part of the government, you're going to find compensation anywhere but the federal government, then?

Eric

Exactly. And as I said, people who don't feel they want to partic-ipate in capitalism or Laborism, we'll leave them alone. Just pay your reduced taxes and enjoy your life.

Phil

But back to the free school . . . people who are going to a govern-ment college and pay nothing except a day of labor each week?

Eric

Exactly. Because our taxes will pay for the rest.

Phil

I understand that, but what does a person—say it's a college kid—do to return the cost of or investment in their education?

Eric

Ideally, the goal is that they use the education. They don't owe anything at the end of receiving their education. Their cost is simply to work a day a week coordinated by the school while they receive their education.

A lot of people already work while they are in college. And preferably, they'd be working in the field they are studying or something complementary to that, but maybe not. Just like college students have always done, those who work while in school under American Laborism may not be working at what their eventual "goal" job would be. That's common when you work and go to school. Some people find a way to intern in a position that directly relates to their field of study, and other people choose to work in other fields.

That's not all bad, either. If you want flexibility or to try something different, that can work in your favor.

Phil

Yeah, but how many people are going to a state-funded college? If this program were implemented and you have a ridiculous number of people taking advantage of it (because you'd be stupid not to), where are these millions of kids going to work for their service?

Eric

I have to point something out. By asking this kind of question, it comes across to me that you're conceding American Laborism is possible. You're now working on logistics. Your brain is trying to work out something that seems like a snag, a shortcoming, or a bottleneck. But what's coming across is that you're thinking of real human beings being impacted by this, and—here's my take— you're solving problems for them.

We've been talking about college but expand the view a little. American Laborism is about educational advancement as a broader concept, specifically intended to maximize the value of someone's labor.

When you think about college, which many people probably do, that can make sense. Pursue a degree, get a job in that field.

But education isn't just college. Some people will need to learn to read, write, and communicate. You can agree that if you can't read and write and communicate, but you learn to, that could improve how much your labor is worth.

Other people may just need better math skills. Or business skills. Or a trade. There might be people who want to work for themselves, and some education is the only thing holding them back. Some may pursue certifications in technology. It could be bookkeeping classes or nursing school. Imagine working in an office and needing more schooling to be promoted to manage other people. We can offer that, and this person can now level up their responsibilities and income.

How many people can we help increase the value of their labor by giving them more training or certificates? Some might be in high school. Some might be looking for a second career. Some might be teens looking for their first job. It might even be people who aren't happy or satisfied in their current line of work, and we give them the ability to pick up different skills.

And really, since this is a safety net offered to everyone but is likely taken up by needy people, how many of them will fit the mold of current college students? Most likely, this will initially appeal to people who are in shelters for whatever reason and can benefit from a structured path toward meeting their needs and improving their skills or education.

Now that this picture is in your mind of a broader variety of people than simply college kids going to established colleges and building American Laborism around them, let's talk about what they're all going to do beyond a day of labor each week to pay for what they receive.

To that I answer . . . they'll be part of an economy that will create more jobs than anyone can imagine.

Remember I said we're going to be taking care of one another? If you ask the federal government for help and want to participate in this, you're not paying for any of your basic needs yourself. Instead, you're going to pitch in to help other students or other people in the community. That could be in the form of taking your turn teaching or feeding or cleaning or building something, offering security services, caring for children, or administrative work.

The presumption of American Laborism is that the trade-off may not be perfect, but it will be acceptable. If your path out of homelessness requires you to harvest fruit or repair potholes, clean windows, answer phones on a helpline, or tutor people who can benefit from your knowledge, we'll identify those jobs and fill them.

Phil

There might be concerns about students who may not fully utilize the educational system provided. Say some people are unmotivated or unproductive but seek free education—how many of them will realistically take on jobs based on what they've studied? It raises the question of follow-through after obtaining the education.

Eric

Sounds like after-college life now for a lot of people . . . except minus the massive loans. There's no way to know, obviously, how many people will be in that situation. Every school and college that participates, plus our own purpose-built schools, will have to find a balance between the jobs and services we need, whether cooking or sweeping or something like that. Don't forget, the labor requirement people provide to get their benefits ends when they graduate or leave school. Then they're free to work wherever they want . . . just like today.

And we're talking about people who are having to find their way in the world right now, right? Whether it's flipping burgers or working in retail or skilled jobs such as carpenter, builder, or electrician, everybody has something to offer while contributing labor. After that, they do whatever they want . . . but they're educated, they're not in debt, and their labor is worth more.

Phil

What's the balance between existing schools and colleges that want to sign up for this and how many new schools will need to be created? Existing schools have inertia, so to speak—classrooms, administrators, educators, processes, and procedures. Even if you think super-pragmatically, they have cafeterias and maybe even connections to the community for jobs, and so forth.

Newly built schools don't have that, but they do have an opportunity to leave out the legacy systems that aren't as good as they could be. They can be built assuming some students need room and board or could even include housing for whole families. New schools can also integrate new teaching methods and technology disruptors. They can work in our favor rather than against us if we build it that way.

So where do we balance the fast start of existing schools and maybe the improvement of new schools, considering we may have millions of people who want the benefits?

Eric

We certainly have to keep going until we find that balance. We will find it over time, but another asset is those potential millions of people—everybody has something to offer. If we wake up tomorrow and there are thirty million people showing up for school, saying, "This is wonderful; I want my free education," that would be something we would have to deal with in each college. We might even task the military to help build facilities and organize people.

Phil

Each school will have to work their way through what we need from these people, so that we can balance this out. And you have to wonder also what the balance of existing students who migrate into the system is, and how many absolutely new students we get.

Eric

Great point. Because someone transferring might take less resources to get up to speed than someone coming in brand new.

Phil

And I don't expect we'll have every person in their perfect role on day one. But I also believe this is a growth opportunity worth starting.

Eric

Let's say someone shows up with absolutely no skills, and they try their hand at cooking, cleaning, sewing, or gardening on the grounds of the campus, or something like that, and it just absolutely doesn't work. Then they'll keep rotating through and finding something else.

Phil

Are you saying that each student would provide a service to their respective school?

Eric

Yes and no . . . to anywhere in the community that the school arranges. The school might be the most obvious and straightforward solution, but we don't have to be limited to that. Local governments, cities, or even states might decide to coordinate with schools for what best matches their needs and the skills of the people contributing.

Phil

Because if you have a population of Penn State going to school for free, are you going to put fifty thousand kids to work around the school? What happens when a new class comes in?

Eric

Well, not to nitpick, but that's a state school. So the state and the college or university will decide whether they even want to participate in this. Besides, schools will be everywhere. Every level of education will have to compete against a "free" option, but as you said, it's not really free. You're participating in Laborism with your labor, but the state and private schools will now be competing against the federal government in educating. And they'll be doing so without any possibility of students getting federal student loans, because federal student loans won't exist anymore.

Phil

But federal funds are still used to support state schools, right?

Eric

We're starting to really focus on college kids again, but they aren't the only people who will want to receive education. But to keep on that thread, yes, the federal government helps fund state universities, assuming the school meets federal guidelines and requirements, and, if it's a private institution, assuming the school doesn't opt to remain independent.

But yes, the notion of federal funding will change when government-guaranteed student loans stop. Moreover, we could look at this town by town, based on the needs of a particular area. For example, do we need a federally funded college in Manhattan, or do we need one in the most rural part of Alaska? Those would probably need to be different, and the federal government could partner with local experts and administrators to maintain those federal guidelines around receiving funds.

Phil

Back to the students. I really want to go through this. What if you're focused on your studies and have trouble with the different levels of learning? What if you're a full-time student and you're working up to full-time hours outside of school? What if working at or for the school, even one day per week, is a challenge?

Eric

We have that now, don't we? Right now, in our world, we have people who learn faster and some who learn slower. We can accommodate that. But the safety net obligation is a day of labor for unlimited school. If someone genuinely can't make full-time school work with one day of contributing back, perhaps they need to lighten their school load by a day, just like students do now. They find that balance.

And all of this is assuming that the person wants to be in the Laborism school system. If they really don't want to or can't contribute a day of labor, but they want to go full time, perhaps a private or state school is better for them.

Phil

Because under the old system, they may not have had to work since maybe federal loans fund their schooling, right? And they're fully participating in their education, as many kids aren't working during school because they have a loan that they're dealing with and allocating that throughout the year instead of working, right?

Eric
Right.

Phil

So, what are these kids who used to get loans going to do, or what are any kids going to do if they are in college and have to provide this work schedule one-to-one ratio of actual, not labor, but service?

Eric

To get benefits, you'll work one day a week and be educated at least one day a week. But that's a minimum on the education— you can enroll full time.

Phil

So then, are you compensating the school? You know, you're getting a free education out of this, or are you giving a free education's worth of work back to that school?

Eric

In this system, we're getting away from expecting someone to always fully fund an education that is designed to improve them with their labor. It's not merely a transaction, it's a benefit.

Phil

But if someone is only working part-time, one day a week, school can cost upward of what, $30,000 a year?

Eric

Right. And maybe let's use that figure of $30,000 . . . maybe the labor you provide wouldn't immediately be considered equivalent to $30,000. That's possible. I'm willing to believe that, but also, you may have someone with higher skills and participation—but even that doesn't matter. And I don't want to always answer this with the minority examples. I would imagine this Advancement

Department, if someone says, "OK, I'd like to participate in this at the federal level, I'm a safety net person, right? I don't have any money to offer, but I want to get educated so I can grow." This is the person we're talking about, right? I show up for school and don't want to take out debt? I don't want loans. And yet, I also didn't qualify for a scholarship. This safety net is therefore a federal scholarship if you carry a little of the load. It can feel transactional, as in exchange labor for benefits—but it can be a little labor for unlimited benefits.

Phil

Explain that. Transactional?

Eric

We're changing the system. We may have to invent a school in our minds that accepts tuition, *but more importantly, it accepts* people. *Someone with no money approaches this school and enrolls. The school signs them up, provides food and housing if needed, and tries to match that student's abilities to a job that needs doing. That might be a job the school needs to have done or something in the community, and the school arranges that, much like colleges arrange work-study programs or internships now. And, of course, the school has a budget, and the federal government funds them for whatever isn't covered by students contributing.*

Phil

Let's look at it differently. What we're saying is that our society has people who need a safety net. At the most basic level, they need food and shelter. Even though America spends outrageous amounts of money to solve this today, we still have the problem.

American Laborism can then solve the safety net problem.

We're redefining the role of the federal government in the safety net.

I'm walking through this because I'm getting to a point.

The American Laborism safety net isn't about money; it's about labor . . . and the expectation that education can improve labor.

Our safety net now becomes—in a nutshell—if a person needs food and shelter, they will get it. The trade-off is that while you receive this, you agree to contribute a day of labor and attend a day of school for each week of benefits you receive. Out of a seven-day week, one goes to helping and one goes to education, and the other five days are yours to do anything you want.

There's also the alternative that you can apply to join the military if that's a better fit for you. And really, nothing has to change with the military, because they already ensure that every soldier, sailor, pilot, or marine receives food and shelter or is paid and can get it themselves.

That brings us to the "what if this works" scenario—what if all forty million needy Americans want to participate in this? Well . . . that's forty million people who start becoming less needy. They aren't just being fed and given shelter. Years down the road, everyone who has asked for help will be better educated and have work experience from however long they were part of this.

As soon as someone asks for help, they start making progress toward perhaps not *needing help. The end is then an educated, experienced, and even independent society.*

What happens in the middle, in-between starting and succeeding? Does America open its doors and let people willing to agree to this deal come and have it?

It makes sense that being able to say yes to this is fundamental to believing it can work. We can't roll out a system that breaks if or when it becomes popular.

Imagine pitching this to Salesforce, a sophisticated

customer-relationship management provider. Since the biggest companies in the world rely on Salesforce to organize customer information, they could easily create a platform for us.

Next, Salesforce partners with ID.me, which offers a digital wallet that interacts with everyone, from the IRS to pharmacies to private businesses. This system is already in place and working.

Integrate the best learning and testing modules both for in-person and remote teaching. In time, we'll need this to be robust because we will have to address teaching people at every level of education. Pre-kindergarten through advanced degrees. Artificial intelligence advances can help with this.

And weave into all that, organizing a growing workforce. If the premise is "What if this works?," then for everyone who needs help, we have someone—the same person—who is providing help. Each person is getting *help* in one area and giving *help in* another. Managing this will take the best hiring and job services and companies in America.

Clearly, we'll need a moonshot gathering of American companies who can onboard people, help them get organized, and guide them toward appropriate education and suitable work.

And of course, the whole platform will have to flow with people advancing their education or work experience. That's why Salesforce could be instrumental in this; they already flow with the changing needs of people.

All this is to say it's not hard to imagine this working just with the tools that we already have.

Eric

You just solved the yes-no-yes framework I have for when someone smart hears a new, good idea for the first time.

In this case, we propose American Laborism as a way to reduce taxes, shrink government, strengthen the military, and *eliminate involuntary poverty in America. Good idea? Yes.*

But then comes the no *part of yes-no-yes: No, American Laborism won't work. You can't offer better services and lower taxes. People won't want to work for benefits. It sounds like wishful communism . . . until the rest of the facts are considered.*

That's where the closing yes *comes in. Yes, by eliminating waste, we can give better services that cost less. By people gaining education and contributing labor, which is always improving because of that same education, it will work. It's not handouts. It's not charity. It's respecting the value of someone's labor.*

That was a broad, wide-ranging conversation that did cover some details, and it was representative of one of the many, many conversations we've had as we've hashed out our ideas for American Laborism. This chapter brought up a lot of big ideas, but there are still details we have to cover, so let's talk about some specifics.

CHAPTER 4

YOU CAN THINK OF LABORISM AS A TAX SYSTEM IF IT HELPS YOU

IN THIS CHAPTER, let's shift gears, but we'll begin with our conversation format.

Phil
How long do you think it would take to pay off government debt? Because I think that is an ambitious task.

Eric
I agree.

Phil
You could say it will never happen if we keep running a deficit, spending more money than our taxes bring in.

Eric
True. The debt is getting bigger, and there's no arguing this out-of-control spending well beyond America's tax revenue is an example of America not taking care of Americans. Every year, we hand our future generations more debt. But I want to save the deficit talk and how long it will take to pay off our debts for later in the conversation. I think now we should discuss the American Laborism aspect of taxes.

Phil
Well, anything affecting people's taxes is already a big deal, but this is even bigger—affecting the entire economic system.

Eric

I agree. So how big can this get? And are there different varieties of this that need to be implemented? Because the difference between what's written in the pages of a book and what happens on the streets when people try to follow that book's ideas . . . well, we're not living in the capitalism that Adam Smith wrote about. And neither are people who live in communist countries living anything at all like what Karl Marx dreamt about. Neither of those in implementation worked out to be at all what the book suggested.

Phil

Would you say there are people who think they are capitalists or Marxists and yet aren't living like what they claim to be?

Eric

What's the old joke—"You can pretend to be a Marxist . . . thanks to capitalists"?

Phil

But American Laborism and the vision for taxes are different from both of those. Will each side immediately see something they like in Laborism?

Eric

As counterintuitive as this is, I'd bet there are people against our tax plan, even though it lowers taxes. It's probably going to be tough to sell because we'll find out pretty quickly who's not paying 10 percent in taxes, and we'll also find out how many people like to punish wealth with progressive taxes. One of our uphill battles will be to convince people that it isn't in their best interest to attempt to bring down successful people, to level the playing field by taxation.

Capitalism and Marxism neglect to specifically lay out workable expectations and limitations for taxation—and are therefore doomed to eventual failure.

That's because taxation is a very simple concept that can quickly become extremely complicated—with devastating results—if you allow it to.

Any humans who form societies and choose to pool their resources will inevitably attempt to finance debt and weave social expectations into the tax code. It's important to remember that the government can only pay for things by charging us taxes or printing more money. So every time you hear the phrase "the government will pay for it," realize the money is coming out of *your* pocket.

Capitalists know intuitively that some taxes are necessary for providing services we all benefit from, but—if I can use a blanket statement—they also believe taxes should be as low as possible, because, in their mind, capital that remains with the people instead of shipped off to politicians and bureaucrats is better.

Let us be clear: if you believe yourself to be a capitalist but you also want to see a high level of government-provided services paid for with high tax brackets, you aren't a capitalist. Just because you want capitalism for yourself doesn't make you a capitalist.

Marxists generally believe that high levels of services and government involvement in people's daily lives require higher taxes to pay for higher services. And if you want more government involvement and higher levels of services, this might make sense to you.

But then we have the dilemma of what taxes to charge the poorest people. Many people believe it's unfair to charge taxes to people with the lowest incomes and the least wealth.

Pursuing that, tax rates under both capitalism and Marxism then necessarily rise for the people who *do* pay taxes to make up for those who *do not*.

And as tax rates rise, so does the incentive for people to avoid paying taxes by any means necessary. Loopholes, gamed systems, cheating . . . there are even numerous documented cases of wealthy people leaving a country in order to pay lower taxes elsewhere.

Two things happen, and they are as inevitable as sinking in quicksand. First, societies gradually come to want more and more things from their government and begin to demand them. Second, people are always looking for ways to minimize their own taxes (which thereby increases the tax burden of others).

It's a disgusting side of human behavior, and it is only possible because the economic systems that cannot avoid participating in taxation have not specified exactly what will be permissible and what won't be at the outset.

American Laborism, by contrast, has fixed federal taxes at its core for both people and companies or organizations who pay taxes. And it isn't just the *rate* that's fixed at 10 percent until the United States national debt is paid off and 2 percent thereafter plus 0.25 percent annually on everything owned. What's also fixed is that everyone will pay the same taxes, because Laborism believes and codifies that literally all citizens and legal residents are equals.

That means that, under American Laborism, there is no federal tax system in which people are taxed at different rates based on their income levels. What is most critical to note is that there is no redistribution of wealth from the rich to the poor. Instead, everyone keeps 90 percent of their income and 99.75 percent of their wealth. Rather than wealthy people paying more so we can maintain the illusion that the money is benefiting poor people, and rather than defining poor people by how much capital they have, providing in-kind benefits increases the benefits and reduces the cost to society of those benefits.

If you can't believe that in-kind benefits and a tax rate that is not progressive are good ideas, take a look at how poorly a progressive tax and cash benefits have done in solving the poverty problem in America.

Taxes that aren't progressive are not a new idea. Often referred to as *flat* taxes, they've been debated in America for years. If a flat tax doesn't appeal to you, perhaps consider the possibility that a tax that "seems fair," in the way a progressive tax seems to cost more for wealthy people, has been tried and failed, whereas a tax that *is* fair—a flat tax—can immediately solve the problems that progressive taxes have not.

Then consider whether there is any possibility that people who prefer progressive taxes are not actually attempting to solve society's problems as much as they are perhaps attempting to enact some kind of wealth transfer, success punishment, or even a perception of leveling the playing field. None of these things has ever worked, and it's time we were honest enough to admit that.

We live in a country wealthy enough to have glistening cities and yet the progressive tax rates haven't solved the wealth inequality gap.

We fully expect this single rule to be the most contentious aspect of American Laborism. Ironically, the biggest resistance will likely be by those who get the most benefit from Laborism and also pay the least in taxes.

That's the horrifying side effect of undefined taxes we will avoid.

Granted, it seems like common sense to create a tax system that taxes people who make more money at a higher rate than those who make less. Something about that feels like it's fair—but fair in the "unequal but somehow justified" sense.

American Laborism, however, believes in fairness in the literal sense. And more importantly, all Americans are equal in the equality sense. There should be no difference in how the federal government treats anybody. None whatsoever—and that includes taxation.

Make no mistake, people who earn more will indeed pay more. If Alice earns ten times as much income as Bob, she will pay ten times as much in tax. If Carlos owns fifty times as much property as

Deborah, he will pay fifty times as much in wealth tax.

There will be no loopholes, and there will be no more apocryphal stories of billionaires who pay a lower rate than their secretary because we will all pay exactly the same rate.

We mentioned in chapter 1 that ownership or wealth taxes have failed in Europe. We don't think our 0.25 percent annual ownership tax will fail, because at the same time we roll it out, we are also cutting the top federal income tax even for the wealthiest people to just 10 percent (who face a top marginal bracket of 37 percent now) and eventually 2 percent once our debt is paid off. If you move out of America, America loses over a 0.25 percent tax on your wealth each year while you enjoy significantly lower income taxes, your leaving is a price we'll have to pay to fix many other issues we face.

If this is the first time you have encountered the idea of a fair non-progressive tax, I encourage you to mull it over as you read these pages.

THIS MAY BE INITIALLY CONTROVERSIAL, but yes, American Laborism means even the lowest earners in our society will be expected to pay taxes. We know this may not be popular, but it is the fair thing to do.

We cannot succumb to the emotional and insultingly degrading concept that "poor people can't pay" and enact laws and policies as if people with lower incomes are some kind of pitiful, helpless participants in a society designed for the benefit of other people. We will not exclude people who earn less money from the opportunity and responsibility to contribute. We can't reiterate nor restate too many times that everyone is equal under American Laborism. There are no Americans who are incapable of participating, contributing, and living a respected, dignified, tax-paying life.

Progressive taxes—literally taxes that charge some people proportionally more than others—divide people. Any federal government that does not take action to protect all its citizens from inequality and division is not legitimate and should be removed from power.

Lastly, if you find yourself repulsed by the idea that we are all equal in the eyes of the federal government, and you are instead eager to inflict progressive "make the wealthy pay a higher rate for the good of everyone" taxes, you are still welcome to enact crushing taxes at the state level. American Laborism's low taxes are federal only.

But under American Laborism, at the federal level, everyone is equal, and the tax rate they pay is too.

What Does American Laborism Do to Social Security?

We're going to stay intentionally broad and high-level with this section.

Social Security already operates somewhat like a fair tax, except not entirely. Everyone who earns W-2–type wages has Social Security taxes withdrawn from their pay, so in that sense it's a fair tax rather than a progressive tax.

But it's not entirely fair. Rather, it becomes a *regressive* tax, which is also not fair. *Regressive* means higher earners pay less proportionally. That's because of a mechanism built into Social Security called the *wage base*. The simple definition of *wage base* is the amount of an individual's wages that are taxed. You might be surprised to learn that Social Security tax is only deducted from the first $160,000 an individual earns (current as of 2023).

That means if you earn $10,000 of wages, all your wages are subject to Social Security tax, but if you earn $1,000,000 of wages, only one of every six dollars you earn is charged the Social Security tax.

The Social Security Administration is looking into a lot of different ways to change this policy with the goal of making Social Security last longer. If you're interested in this specifically, you can learn more about it at www.ssa.gov.

Truth be told, Social Security doesn't have enough money to pay for all the benefits they've promised people, so some kind of change is needed.

Perhaps that's an understatement. What we should say is that the Social Security system *will* change with or without American Laborism. If we as a country do nothing, Social Security will run out of money. If we agree to change Social Security, there's a good chance people will be upset about it.

As we saw with the massive unrest in France during the spring of 2023, which was caused entirely by proposals to change people's retirement benefits, this isn't easy to pull off.

Here's what you need to know: Americans who earn wages pay a portion of them into the Social Security system. Other Americans (who qualify) can receive benefits from the Social Security system. Oversimplifying the system, we need to put more money in than we are taking out. Put another way, the money *you* are putting into Social Security today immediately goes to pay *someone else's* benefits today—and *your* future benefits payment depends on *other people* putting *more money* into the system when you're at retirement age.

Complicating this is the fact that Americans—for the most part—are living longer. It's common sense that it costs more to pay one generation's thirty years' worth of benefits than it might cost to pay the previous generation's fifteen years' worth of benefits.

Add to that the fact that many people have paid into Social Security for their whole lives, and the idea of having their benefits cut is frightening. And to be honest, it feels unfair.

But the position we're in is that the system has promised more in future benefits than the expected future collections can pay. We have to recognize that unless our lawmakers can come up with a solution, the system will not be able to meet its obligations. We aren't insolvent yet, but if nothing changes, we very well could be.

As for how American Laborism handles Social Security, we believe that a commitment to people who have worked to earn benefits must be met. American Laborism will not end, cut, or replace Social Security. That also means the current payroll tax levied against your paycheck that goes into Social Security will not change either.

Once American Laborism rolls out, the entire Social Security Administration will be folded into the United States Post Office. To us, it makes sense that the USPS, with personnel and facilities in nearly every community around America, can administer Social Security.

However, Social Security's impending insolvency is unacceptable, and something must be done. If properly rolled out, American Laborism can help mitigate the coming stress America will see when we try to "fix" Social Security, because at least everyone will know their basic needs are met thanks to American Laborism.

That may make the sting of increasing payroll taxes, rising wage bases, and/or deferred retirement easier to bear. Those are the options that lawmakers are considering. It's also possible that benefit-increase freezes could be deployed, but that would also be unpopular.

By now it should be clear that American Laborism does not offer a prescription for ending, changing, or even improving Social Security. We do offer a system that—should it be in place when Social Security ends or changes—can alleviate some of the pain people feel when that happens. (We have a section on older folk, the most customary Social Security recipients, following.)

We have some thoughts, though, on how we'd stave off the collapse of Social Security, if you're interested. Because some people have paid into the system for decades and counted on it for their primary source of income during retirement, we'd approach fixing it with a combination of every possible variable.

First, the retirement age needs to shift upward. Not all at once; that would be painful for a lot of people. Perhaps every two years we can increase the retirement age by one month.

Next, we'd eliminate the regressive nature of the Social Security tax itself. As much as we don't think progressive taxes are fair, neither do we think regressive taxes are. We believe an unlimited wage base is fair. Along with that, though, we'd have to address potential future benefits. They'd have to be either outright capped or perhaps rise at a lower rate after a certain point. This will be unpopular, but it must be done.

We would increase the current withholding amount, but only by a small amount—perhaps as little as a 1 percent increase. If you take the next step, a bigger increase than that won't be necessary.

We'd recommend a completely transparent and radical change to how the Social Security trust funds are invested. Imagine it like a sovereign wealth fund, with the charter of investing in the best American companies. We'd implement strict investment criteria, such as only investing in companies who display respect for labor, treat their employees well, and hire people participating in the labor requirement of receiving benefits.

We can't go any deeper into this subject without writing another book, but you can see that we believe Social Security can be saved if America begins making tough and potentially unpopular decisions.

On the other hand, if we don't fix Social Security, in a decade there will be millions of people who will immediately need the safety net of American Laborism when Social Security collapses.

Now, a final thought on taxation. It's time to put an end to the practice of using taxation as a way to take money from one person to give to another. It is impossible for individuals to be both equals and wards of other individuals at the same time.

Laundering, sterilizing, and anonymizing the payments by washing them through a bloated bureaucracy does nothing to remove the fact that taking money from one person by threat of force and giving it to another person because they supposedly deserve it is legalized theft.

And it has to end.

WE MENTIONED ONE REASON Social Security is under pressure is that people are living longer. That's generally been true for the past century. However, the Centers for Disease Control and Prevention statistics point out a disheartening decline in life expectancy since 2019 due to drug overdose and COVID-19 deaths.[11]

Another part of the equation is that Americans are having fewer babies. That means fewer people are entering the workforce and contributing to Social Security at the same time benefits are lasting longer as people withdraw from Social Security since they're living longer.

We mention this not to present the doom and gloom scenario of fewer young workers supporting a growing number of retirees, but rather to present an optimistic daydream we allow ourselves.

And that is, we'd like to imagine that families who may have thought the economic challenges of having more kids is too much might reconsider if they knew about American Laborism. How many families, couples, and individuals might opt to form or grow their families if they knew they were at no risk of ever living without necessities?

How many families would see American Laborism as a way for the caregiver to work a small amount, pursue further education, and still have most of their time available for their family?

This daydream is beyond statistics, we'll admit, but we certainly feel in our heart of hearts that it's possible.

American Laborism, therefore, could re-energize the American family.

CHAPTER 5

CAPITALISM FAILED BECAUSE NOT EVERYONE HAS CAPITAL

CAPITALISM IS AN *economic* system, not a *political* system. Liberals and conservatives, left and right, Republicans, Democrats, Libertarians, Greens, and even anarchists may not agree on much . . . but they can all be capitalists. A textbook will tell you that capitalism is when the industries and the "means of production" are privately owned. That simply means investors, corporations, and entrepreneurs own the businesses that make things for us, rather than the government.

Capitalism believes that individuals should be able to buy goods and services at prices set by the market, rather than by the government. As goods and services are sold, a seller can produce more goods, buy more equipment, or hire more labor. If the goods and services are sold for more than what it costs to produce them, the seller can net a profit and start to accumulate capital.

So capitalists aim to accumulate capital.

It's really that simple. If you live in a world that is based on having capital, and you yourself don't have any capital, you will be at a disadvantage and unable to participate. Possibly forever.

Capitalists, when attempting to account for someone with no capital wanting to participate in the free market or invest or improve their finances, the answer is almost always, "Convert your labor into capital, and then you can participate in capitalism."

That's right—capitalists' answer to not having any capital is "get a job."

Which means labor must be the bedrock foundation upon which capitalism is built, and by overlooking that—perhaps intentionally—capitalists with capital build in the delay that people with no capital must overcome before they can participate.

Moreover, imagine that there are people who have no capital, and the product of their earnest labor is not enough to set aside capital. This is one place where the concept of "the rich get richer" comes from.

There's nothing wrong with the rich getting richer . . . unless they're doing it by making others poorer or—as many people believe—pulling up the ladder so others have a harder time making their own wealth. This is the reputation capitalism has.

Unfortunately for those who truly believe in capitalism, there are two inescapable facts that the entire world can see, and merely believing in capitalism is not enough to refute them.

First, capitalism hardly seems fair when it's easy to see the extremes of wealth and poverty coexisting under capitalism, sometimes separated by mere miles. It's not uncommon to see wealthy neighborhoods situated just a few minutes away from the more poverty-stricken areas.

The American Laborism response to those with wealth is not to attack or bring them down. Rather, the "big idea" at the core of Laborism is to sustainably bring everyone from the bottom up, without bringing anyone else down.

Second, anyone seeing that wealth gap and looking for an alternative economic system to capitalism that may promise more fairness will undoubtedly consider Marxism, such as the numerous focus–group-named varieties of socialism or the idealistically named communism. These are all systems that have been tried in the past and have failed.

We'll talk about why Marxism fails in the next chapter. And we don't need to pretend that any new arguments must be raised against capitalism, because as much as we want it to work, America has been attempting capitalism for generations, and we have the largest wealth inequalities we've ever had. Even with all our advances, something isn't working right if the wealthiest people in our country continue to hold such a disproportionate amount of money. But here's the scary part: We have tens of millions of Americans living in poverty. If we change nothing, we can't expect the huge population in poverty to change, can we? What we, as the authors, are worried about is that nothing changes . . . and the population living in poverty grows even larger. Imagine condemning someone to poverty just so we can keep everything status quo.

And frankly, like the traveler finding themselves in Australia when their destination was Austria, we need to realize that we didn't end up where we intended, even though our complex system of thousands upon thousands of laws may make it feel like we've made progress since our founding. It's hard to believe that America is doing right by Americans when we see so many people in poverty in a wealthy country.

We've all heard about people who work extremely hard day in and day out just to make ends meet. Good-hearted people who want to help those who are struggling believe that raising the minimum wage will somehow solve this problem.

It's pleasant to think about, for sure, that giving all low-wage laborers a raise will "catch them up" to some imaginary suitable lifestyle. But it will never happen, because without a government willing and able to freeze the prices of literally everything in the country except for labor, the price of goods will simply rise as the minimum wage rises.

However, it is important to consider what happens when someone is willing to provide their labor but feels that their labor is not valued as much as they would like, so they pursue advancing their training or education.

Even if not every individual increases the value of their labor by seeking more education, it's impossible to believe anything other than most—if not nearly all—who *want* to earn more *can* earn more if they increase their education.

This is why American Laborism provides free, lifetime, unlimited education. It makes sense that anyone who wants to improve their circumstances (yes, even if it is merely to achieve higher wages) should be given that opportunity.

This is a fundamental belief of American Laborism—that everyone has something valuable to contribute to society through their labor.

Yes, *everyone*.

Now, before we move on, it's important to clarify in no uncertain terms that we will not suffer fools with extreme outlier examples. We're confident that someone reading this right now is scrambling through their mind to imagine an edge case of an imagined person who, for whatever reason, wouldn't have the ability to contribute.

We'll make it easy for those eagerly trying to "gotcha" American Laborism: we'll stipulate that, yes, there are cases of people who don't immediately appear to have valuable labor to contribute, but that doesn't mean they don't have value.

People in comas come to mind.

We'll concede there may be other examples. The fundamental belief of American Laborism is that every person is to be treated equally and that everyone has something of value to contribute.

They don't need to contribute labor on behalf of anyone else. They don't need to contribute labor at all—unless they want federal benefits, that is. For every critic who believes we are wrong in our thinking and that there must be a lot of people who are nothing but takers and have no value to themselves, we would counter that for every one of those imaginary examples, there are likely a dozen people who lack just one test or one class to graduate or one certification to unlock a better job, an immediate raise, or even the ability to start their own company.

So for everyone who wants to argue that "American Laborism will fail because someone maybe can't work," we say it will succeed because there are so many more people who are ready to benefit immediately from it.

But back to capitalism failing those without capital . . . and American Laborism solving that.

By making education available to everyone who wishes to gain more of it, we will immediately increase the value of their labor. The fundamental flaw of capitalism is that the on-ramp to acquiring capital is out of reach for a great many people. If you already have a lot of money, you don't need an on-ramp.

But Americans with little to no capital can increase their education, raise the value of their labor, and if they choose to, cash in their labor for higher pay, live within their means, and on-ramp themselves to where they can participate in capitalism.

But it's obvious that without Laborism and unlimited, free education, for many people, that on-ramp doesn't exist.

Don't try to argue that it does. *Of course* it does—*for some people.*

But under American Laborism, that on-ramp is available for *everyone.*

We'll finish this chapter with a last thought about American capitalism. America has so much capital that it can literally be a challenge for investors, money managers, venture capitalists, and the like to find places to invest their capital. Look no further than overvalued or quickly funded public offerings or startups—if capital were scarce, we would never see that. We literally have plenty of capital.

Now, imagine if we were to change the foundation of our country and economy to labor rather than capital. Our best investors and entrepreneurs would then scramble to train and employ the greatest number of people—a resource with a limited supply.

But capitalism hasn't just failed theoretically or because not everyone has capital. Capitalism has failed in another way in that it's now affecting our government.

Let's go back to our conversation where the subject of how capitalism—our economic system—has perhaps tainted our society and how it interacts with our government.

Phil

So, how will American Laborism change the wealth already distributed in terms of monopolies and government handouts, and specific government agencies in business with major companies that are basically pulling all the strings of the world at this point? How does anything change that?

Eric

They'll have to offer their services to the Advancement Department, Military Department, or Post Office and compete in the open marketplace—or compete for a small piece of a very small federal budget. Obviously, we can't just immediately cancel all government purchasing contracts. But as we shrink the government— and also begin to publicly track all government expenditures—the handouts, earmarks, and contracts will shrink.

Phil

And you think these people will be like, "Ah, nah, we're good"?

Eric

They don't have that choice.

Phil

OK. Who's implementing it then?

Eric

The executive branch of the federal government.

Phil

Which is going to say, "We're going to downsize, and we're going to take our own power away from us and give it back to the people"?

Eric

Absolutely. Some programs can be shifted to states or regions, or maybe even other countries, if appropriate. But the federal government of this country will severely limit what it's involved in and shift to something sustainable and fair for everyone.

Phil

I like how that sounds, sure. Who doesn't want our government less able to pump billions of dollars into companies? But let's say you're a scientific lab, and your only customer is the government. Yet what you're offering doesn't add value that the new American Laborism government needs. Maybe nothing in educational advancement, the military, or the post office needs your lab.

Eric

You might be out of luck. You may have to find another patron. This is how we got to where our federal government spends trillions upon trillions of dollars, and just about everyone who lives here feels like they're not getting their money's worth.

Phil

Even some people who don't pay taxes feel like they're not getting their money's worth from the government.

Eric

American Laborism will reverse that. We can talk more about taxes later, but we're going to shift this around to where everybody knows that everybody else is paying exactly the same amount. And if that leaves some organizations, some companies, some scientific labs, some employees out . . .

Phil

. . . *basically, what is healthy about companies, capitalists, and people who benefit from this bloated budget, right?*

Eric

Our system needs to stop catering to them. And that may sound harsh, but . . . well . . . our system does need to stop catering to them. Our system needs to find a way to let them know that we don't answer to them. We have been, and changing that is going to be difficult, but here's a concept that maybe we could explore, because I know there's been a lot written about the so-called tyranny of the minority.

Is that what we're talking about here? Is that the bureaucrats, or the kleptocrats, or the people living off the fat of the land, or who maybe aren't producing?

Those organizations have worked us into where the bureaucrats and the system as it is doesn't represent everybody, and yet we're all having to work in a system that benefits a small number of people the most—whether it's a private company that's getting beneficial contracts, or even if it's an individual who shows up for work every day and doesn't accomplish anything. I don't think there's that many of them, but we can't hold back society for them regardless.

Phil

You know you just said American Laborism can not only fix bloated budgets but can give us the free education and world-class military? Seems like when you talk about replacing capitalism with American Laborism and fixing where capitalism fails us— where our government fails us—the benefits will outweigh that.

Eric

That's deep. I like that. America used to be such that everyone was left so much alone that the very small amount of federal govern-ment interaction anyone had certainly benefited them more than the cost of the government. I'm thinking in the railroad-building days when America was growing. The federal government didn't build railroads, I know that—but the job of the government was international trade and commerce, and maybe to ensure that we had a sound currency and laws that progressively treated one another fairer over time. And we all thought, "OK, the govern-ment is doing its job."

Phil
Americans probably didn't begrudge having a government as much when it was small.

Eric
But now we've worked our way into a situation where, like you said, even people who don't pay for government, who don't pay taxes, feel they're not getting their money's worth. And the ques-tion is, well, what about these people who receive income from taxes? Those can't be the people we're solving for, because that's who got us here. We're now under their thumb, and we need to get out of that. And if it takes saying something as inflammatory as the government needs to focus on people who need help, at the expense of huge budgets and massive contracts, and the employees who have been taking for a long time, then that's what's going to have to happen. Might not be popular with them, but we'll find out.

Phil
I'm not worried. I think we'll find more people in America who believe it's important to care for the least of those among us. The people who need the help the most.

CHAPTER 6

MARXISM FAILS BECAUSE SOME PEOPLE DO HAVE CAPITAL

MARXISM IS A SOMEWHAT convenient naming of the incredibly broad-ranging economic and philosophical writings of Karl Marx and Friedrich Engels. While capitalism is purely an economic system, Marxism is that *plus* a social and political system. In that respect alone, it's vastly different from capitalism.

But there's another, far greater difference. Marxism believes that capitalism leads to inequality and, therefore, attempts to create a society where the ownership of the means of production are shared. Exactly *what* is shared and with *whom* can vary depending on whether we're talking about a theoretical ideal of Marxism or one of the numerous Marxist, communist, or socialist governments who have tried it.

Quite often, the simple theory of "shared means of production" requires a strong central government to maintain, which can, in turn, focus the ownership of the supposedly shared resources into a few fortunate hands rather than equally spread out among the entire populace. Truth be told, over history there are numerous examples of the "sharing," enriching some folks and quite literally starving others.

Even though Marxism has been tried multiple times before and failed every time, there are still people who believe in it. Oftentimes, those failures end up being very violent and tragic.

Still, the idea of equality, an equal outcome, or an equal lifestyle for everyone is appealing to many people. And no doubt, seeing the huge gap between the haves and have-nots living in most capitalist societies makes Marxism's promise of equality, living wages, and generous government programs for all seem tempting.

Given that American Laborism has promised to lower taxes and offer unlimited, free education, it's not surprising that some people might be tempted to make lazy comparisons between American Laborism and Marxism.

In fact, if a critic of American Laborism is willing to be intellectually dishonest enough to claim that it is like communism, in which everyone shares equal burden, then throwing around critiques like "free education sounds like Marxism" would certainly satisfy the needs of someone who is too lazy to think for themselves.

We're not denying that unlimited, free education might sound like a too-good-to-be-true offer, like the "everyone receives the same benefits all provided by government" utopian goals of Marxism, if you ignore that our "free" education requires a fair trade-off of the recipient providing some valuable labor.

But this isn't even why Marxism fails!

There are two inconvenient truths that will always spell the demise of Marxism. First, if even only one human participant in a Marxist society wants to break out and work harder and get ahead, they would have virtually no incentive to do so because, in a true "we all receive the same" society, everyone would receive the same regardless of how much harder one person worked.

So Marxism, when it is practiced in the real world, acknowledges that and attempts to accommodate it by allowing some individuals to get ahead.

The second difficult reality about Marxism is that as soon as some people gain some capital under the Marxist system, the idea of everyone having the same amount of resources becomes unattractive to the people who now have more.

It is certainly true that some people become very wealthy under Marxist economics, as they do under capitalist economics—that cannot be denied.

But instead of everyone celebrating the success of the people who have resources and sharing those resources equally—as is the promise of Marxism—the sharing never seems to materialize.

Some people would argue that if certain individuals were not allowed to succeed under Marxism, then innovation, efficiencies, and discoveries that would benefit the population would gradually disappear. That's probably true. But it's also true in capitalism.

So the real argument is that—at least for humans—Marxism, under which *some* folks have huge amounts of capital, looks more like capitalism than it does Marx's Marxism. Furthermore, the people at the bottom of the Marxist-social ladder—those who are supposedly receiving an equal share of what the community produces—never seem to find an on-ramp to success either.

The reason that nobody at the bottom of the Marxist ladder has capital is not because nobody has capital; it's because that is how Marxism works. Capital exists . . . but it stays at the very top.

What's even worse is that their system doesn't even pretend that everyone should have a chance to acquire capital for themselves. Once you're in a Marxist country, you will likely see that a very small number of people control most of the capital.

And then there's the pesky fact that any communal, communist, or Marxist system doesn't take into consideration that not every human wants to participate in their own lives at the same level as everyone else.

Some people simply want to give more and do more and be more.

Phil

American Laborism erases the need for any kind of Marxism because the benefits are a perpetually increasing, educated class with perpetually rising value of labor. Even your lowest member of society who opts into this immediately begins to participate in improvement at their own scale, at their own schedule. But before American Laborism, if I were to just walk up to a stranger on the street and say, "How would you like to live in a society where literally even the lowest members of society, the people who need the most help, are spending every day bettering themselves?," how long would it take for that to become an ideal society or an ideal to work toward?

Eric

No matter how long it takes, you'd imagine they'd see it's worth starting than waiting.

Phil

And if I then said to them, "The cost that we'll have to pay is that some departments will have to merge, and there may be some downsizing among bureaucrats. But what we get out of it is that even the least among us have the dignity to participate on their own, and they're offering that to other members of society."

Eric

That actually doesn't get talked about enough. Maybe it should be. You know, people who get something from society, I would imagine they would welcome the opportunity to feel like "I'm participating by giving back. I'm sharing back."

Phil

That, and there are so many unsung heroes, such as nurses and firemen. We have this understanding in our psyche as Americans (and humans) that there are people out there who share more than they receive.

Eric

I think we probably have an untapped resource of people who would like to be seen that way. "Sure. Take care of my basic needs, and then I'll go out and do two times as much to thank you for that."

Think of a busboy in a typical American family restaurant. I can see someone like that who, when given a job, works ten times harder than you ever thought she or he would. It might be a waitress, a nurse, a mechanic, someone who paints your house, or any number of people like that. You work out a fair deal, they get to work, and then you say, "Wow. This person gave me a lot more than I bargained for."

Phil

I think there's a lot of that out there, and I think there are probably people who haven't been addressed by our society that could be addressed by what American Laborism has to offer.

Eric

It's not that sharing is poison. Americans are good at sharing. But forced *sharing is not American.*

And you can't tell an American we're going to share everything and then give wealth only to people close to the government and poverty only to people who aren't. That's Marxism.

CHAPTER 7

WHY LABOR IS BETTER— FOR EVERYONE— THAN CAPITAL

AFTER ADMITTEDLY PROVIDING a very basic overview of the shortcomings of capitalism and Marxism, we have one final concept to explain in a simplified way.

We believe labor has some special powers that capital just doesn't have. Since everyone already owns their labor, it's on tap to create value for you whenever you choose to use it . . . in an almost magical way. We believe labor, conceptually, is more valuable than capital is.

Phil
So the basic construct of this whole American Laborism system is that people inherently can provide some value or service because of their labor, and not just draw off the system?

Eric
Absolutely.

Phil
And we're shifting the whole safety net and any interaction with the government from the mindset of "trying to beat the government" to "working alongside that government" that is (now) incentivizing us to better our lives?

Eric
I like the way you put that. Plus, people can own *the labor they offer by putting their skills to work. You will always own your own labor.*

Phil

This is at a very basic level, right? Is it at a minimal level?

Eric

Mostly, yes. This is American Laborism at a very basic, minimal level. Of course, there are going to be highly skilled people like scientists, attorneys, inventors, entrepreneurs, professional athletes, and so on, right? And those people can always decide if they want to offer their skills in this system or if they want to go into the private sector themselves.

Phil

Why would a successful lawyer want to go into this new system? Where's the incentive?

Eric

They may not want to. The incentive will be personal for every-body. And, obviously, we started off by talking about solving the needs of the people who need them the most—because this will be the least disruptive economic revolution for people who don't need it ever possible, right? You're not going to have to pick up a weapon and talk a surgeon into participating in this system, because they can say, "It doesn't seem like it's changing much for me other than my taxes going down."

But back to the real point I was trying to make: People starting out—entry level, semi-skilled, skilled, even profes-sionals—their labor is worth something, and that increases as they advance their education.

Phil

It's interesting to me how converting America to an economic system based on labor . . . I don't know how to put this . . .

stretches, *or maybe* refines *our understanding of labor, right? When you think about labor or laborer or respecting labor, what pops into your head? For most people, it's probably someone who works for a wage per hour or maybe is in a union and/or a trade profession. But convert the whole society, all of America, and it's those people plus anyone else. Professionals, doctors, attorneys.*

Eric
It almost becomes difficult to find someone whose labor isn't valuable. Or should I say, someone whose labor doesn't matter.

A young person's first job is often babysitting, a way to earn some money by turning their time and the labor of caring for a child into a job. Other young people, or even adults starting their own business, use their labor to do yard work or deliver newspapers and advertising circulars or perform entry-level restaurant jobs.

The magic of these is that you can start with nothing but the labor you already own and convert your time into a job that earns you money.

Over time, the entry-level employee at a restaurant can become a manager, owner, or even chef if the right skills get advanced. Babysitting can advance into childcare or coaching or teaching over time. Yard work can advance into gardening or landscaping with education and experience.

The labor of an air traffic controller can guide a plane to a safe landing. The labor of a surgeon saves lives. The labor of a carpenter or electrician builds homes for people to live in. The labor of a soldier protects their country. Not only can capital not accomplish any of this, but capital can't start from zero and work its way into saving lives, cooking meals, or building homes.

Sure, some people are born knowing they'll have access to capital, and that's good for them. But not everyone will. On the other hand, everyone is born already owning all their labor. What they choose to do with it and how they choose to advance themselves to make their labor as valuable as it can be is up to them, and we want to make sure everyone can maximize that value.

However, we are confident this chapter will be the dividing point between people who have common sense and those who believe themselves to have *uncommon* sense. That second group is about to start arguing against the possibility that in a country with over three hundred million people, American Laborism doesn't deserve a chance to right the failings of capitalism. With their sharp wit, they'll come up with some n=1 arguments against it.

What does *n=1 arguments* even mean, though?

Simply put, *n=1* is our shorthand for someone attempting to use a sample size of one argument as if it applies to a whole society. It's sort of like thinking every pair of shoes on the store shelf should have an extra shoe with it because there might be someone out there who has three feet. No disrespect intended to anyone who has three feet, but you can easily see how questioning "what about that one person who [fill in the blank]," though considerate, is foolish as well.

Here's how it works when you're trying to improve society: Imagine that rather than voting, you simply give a survey to just one person in your neighborhood from which you'd set a policy that everyone in the neighborhood had to live by.

Already sounds risky, doesn't it? Because one person's beliefs may be very different from what everyone else believes, and they may be very passionate about their views.

But it gets worse. What if the one person in the survey was intentionally selected simply because they were *expected* to be an outlier?

Now, take it to what some folks think is its logical extreme: Let's say you specifically sought out the most difficult person in the entire country and vowed to create laws for more than three hundred million Americans based on what might work for that one most difficult person. Hardly seems honest, right?

Keep that in mind as you read the next sentence, which is perhaps the most critically important belief in American Laborism:

Everyone has valuable labor they can contribute if they desire.

There's a lot to unpack there. Let's get the easy stuff out of the way first by explaining the phrase "if they desire." Yes, American Laborism relies on the notion that people's needs will be met *if they are willing to contribute a fair amount of their labor.*

No, not *all* their labor. A *portion* of their labor. Laborism isn't a full-time job. It isn't a vocation or career. It's a tax system, a safety net, and free lifetime education, and that's it.

As you'll see, we don't expect this contribution of labor to be a direct 1:1 connection to meeting their needs. So if someone has welding skills but needs food and shelter, they wouldn't be asked to weld themselves a home and some food, but they would be provided those things if they were willing to work—possibly welding—where they could do the most good. (Obviously, that's an example. We hardly believe skilled welders will be the ones who need help. Not a chance!)

And yes, contributing is optional for everyone who doesn't ask the federal government for assistance. Once that welder no longer needs help, they are under no further obligation to contribute. Literally come and go as you wish. The only catches are that they contribute some labor, and they participate in education while receiving benefits. (And of course, pay their very low taxes if they are paid for their labor in the free market.)

That also covers the "contribute" part, then, in that the contributions of labor (and being further educated) are simply in exchange for federal assistance and otherwise purely voluntary.

So how can we possibly believe that everyone has valuable labor to contribute?

We can't mean someone who is laid up in a hospital with a broken spine from a recent accident will be put to work, right? Nor could we mean a toddler who can't even speak yet? Or the single mother of that toddler?

This is the crux of the n=1 critique: attempting to find what appear to be valid arguments against trying something that would benefit hundreds of millions of people, simply because there may be a person who doesn't immediately see where and how they fit. We'll cover as many of these "what abouts" as we can think of in the following chapters, because they actually strengthen the pro–American Laborism argument, rather than take it down.

But for now, we'll state unabashedly that yes, we believe literally everyone has valuable labor to contribute.

It may be anything—physical labor, proofreading, sewing, childcare, gardening, nursing, or welding. But not just those; *anything* can be contributed *somewhere*. Like FDR's make-work programs to lift America out of the Great Depression, we'll make up jobs for people if we have to. But we don't expect that to be necessary.

We expect to see a surge in the number of people who find they can teach, mentor, or offer guidance and coaching. Exactly why that is will be made clear in later chapters, but assume it's because millions of new students will need help. It's a fascinating benefit from American Laborism that we're excited to see play out.

Again, everyone has valuable labor they can contribute. And since unlimited education is available to everyone, everyone also has the opportunity to increase the value of their labor if they wish. This is a unique strength of valuing labor: *it's possible to increase how much your labor is worth by advancing your education.*

You can't say that about capitalism! It is not possible to increase the amount of capital someone has merely by educating them; they'll still need to apply that education to something that looks a lot like labor. Even if you attempted to grant everyone access to capital, it wouldn't take long for the capital to return from the hands of the people willing to give up their capital to those who come up with ways to accumulate it.

Simply put, if everyone has valuable labor to contribute, they'll also have labor tomorrow and the following day. And it will be worth more every day if they want it to be.

However . . .

If a skeptic is willing to critique American Laborism, here is where they should do it simply because if the skeptic allows the argument that everyone has valuable labor to contribute if they want to stand, Laborism stands.

So skeptics need to attack that contention. And to do so, they need to claim that not everyone has valuable labor to contribute. This is where doubters have to make their stand and attempt to prove that we are oversimplifying what valuable labor is.

To attack American Laborism, skeptics need to find examples of people who don't fit into our framework.

They might start with someone uneducated, who doesn't have a strong command of any of America's most commonly spoken languages, might be physically challenged, and possesses below-average intelligence.

Surely, the skeptic needs to say right here and right now that they believe the person they described hardly has any valuable labor to contribute.

To which we'd say, first, don't be a jerk. What the skeptic just did . . . is being a jerk. They tried to make an example of someone because they appear to be worth less.

And second, the skeptic is wrong. In their zeal to "what about" American Laborism, they just described someone who knows a language not commonly spoken in America. That sounds valuable, doesn't it?

The military needs people like that. Colleges and publishers value people with language skills like that. If nothing else, they can teach others that language! Don't forget the importance of America's Navajo code talkers during World War II—they were people who knew a language that very few other people knew. They bravely provided their labor and expertise to the US military when it was needed the most.

Hopefully we've made the point that n=1 arguments can be defeated by just one example that contradicts them.

The point of this chapter was to extend the possibility that labor is better than capital for everyone. There's no argument that not everyone has capital, and it should be clear that it's not too much of a stretch to claim that everyone has valuable labor.

Back to our conversation . . .

Phil

We've touched on this a few times, but how do we determine the true value of an individual's labor in terms of the service provided to the federal government, and who gets to decide? For example, say I want to participate in college for a formal education. What labor can I provide? Duration of labor? Terms of labor? Who determines if my labor is equal to my reward?

Eric

That's a fair question, and the answer might surprise you. It doesn't matter. And that's not as ridiculous of an answer as it may sound. Here's the simple explanation: you're not getting paid cash wages, so the wage doesn't matter.

Here's the deeper answer: Everyone from janitor to professor who receives benefits receives the same amount: what they need. Food, shelter, clothing, an opportunity to contribute labor, and either enrollment in the military or free training and education for as long as they want it.

Phil

Therefore, you don't put a value on labor because everyone's the same.

Eric

Unless it isn't—but even then, it still is. What if the janitor has children and the professor does not? Then by Laborism meeting the needs of the janitor's entire family, couldn't you argue they are being paid more? Is that fair to the professor that a janitor gets more needs covered?

But there's a remedy. Remember, Laborism never counts on a person to provide all their available labor just to cover their needs. So if the professor in this example wants to receive more value for their labor, they are welcomed and encouraged to find opportunities to get paid for their labor. Just not from the safety net.

Therefore, the value of your labor, if you're receiving benefits, is the same as everyone else's who is also receiving benefits. As for the duration, as long as you receive benefits, you'll participate in providing labor. The terms are that you'll work with the skills you have, and your compensation will meet your needs.

Phil

And who determines if your labor is worth what you're receiving?

Eric

You do.

If your labor is worth far more in the private sector, and more is what you want, you're encouraged to seek out that higher compensation for your valuable labor.

Phil

You're saying Laborism is counting on the idea that as people

*learn, their labor will rise in value, and they can absolutely take
advantage of that.*

Eric

*Let's talk about that completely free, unlimited benefit of educa-
tion for life. I imagine there will be colleges that join this and
say, "Yes, we'd like to participate in this." We'll continue to refer
to them generally as schools, because they'll include pre-K elementary schools, grammar schools, middle schools, high schools, trade
schools, colleges, and universities.*

Phil

*I'm going to ask for clarification here. Everyone—under American
Laborism—is entitled to unlimited, lifetime free education.
How? Does every school, college, university, medical school, and
Ivy League school just become free overnight? Have they all been
taken over?*

Eric

*No. Not at all. In fact, if they don't want to participate, they don't
have to. We're not going to force any of them to be part of this.*

*So obviously, for that to be true, we have to be ready and
willing to create or build schools or training facilities where
needed. And we'll take full advantage of efficiencies from distance
or remote learning where it makes sense.*

Phil

*Overnight, do we build schools or programs for millions of people?
Who's going to do this?*

Eric

The beneficiaries are, for one. We'll tap the Military Corps of

Engineers. And we'll have millions of square feet of available offices from all the government departments that we trim. And we'll integrate the efficiencies of AI and distance learning where it's possible and effective to do so. We could very well be on the cusp of an educational revolution where every teacher integrates artificial intelligence into their classroom so every student gets a fully customized and personalized curriculum.

But more importantly, as much as possible, we'll partner with schools that want to be part of this. And since we're getting out of the bloated, insanely overinflated federal student loan, grant, and scholarship business, I think we'll find schools eager to support this.

Phil

You think *they will? You're not sure?*

Eric

First and foremost, I care about individuals. If schools have to make a tough decision, that's what they have boards and regents for. If they offer a quality education, but their entire economy crumbles without federal cash, they should have prepared for this. There's never been a guarantee to continue going into debt to pay for things we clearly can't afford.

Phil

What about schools and universities that don't want to partic-ipate in Laborism? I understand there will be basically three different kinds of schools. [For the sake of explanation, as we said before, we're calling everything schools, from preschool all the way to the most advanced universities and technical schools. They're schools.]

Those three kinds are: schools that are completely in the

Laborism federal system; schools that are independent but still participate with Laborism students; and schools that are independent and do not participate.

Eric

Well, our schools are all at the federal level, but obviously will be located within states and municipalities.

States and local municipalities as well as private organizations are also free to maintain their own schools. There will be no expected closing or affecting of private or state schools and universities.

Phil

Back to the question, though: It's unrealistic to wake up and have everyone in school overnight. There must be a transition period.

Eric

Of course. Once we—as a country, that is—decide we're on a course of American Laborism and conversion, the laws and actually implementing this will take some time. A ramp-up period. Maybe we'll get some TikTokers to get everyone excited and make the move over in a year.

And this is also the time that existing schools must prepare for the transition.

Phil

That could cause some serious pain for some universities. Any of them that receive substantial federal aid will have a lot of difficult adjustments to make. Some of them may not even be able to make the transition to life without all those dollars flowing in.

Eric

If every American were already receiving unlimited, free education

—and they are not—I'd have a little more sympathy for schools charging $50,000 a semester.

But I don't.

I care about everyone getting as much education as they need. As far as anyone could ever need, any kind of education will be available or provided, because need doesn't happen at a certain time, right? Need happens at any time. Someone could be young or old and find themselves in need.

And the military, same thing. Obviously, the military will have to have some restrictions in that we won't allow someone who's nine years old to approach the military or Army or Navy or Air Force or Marines or Space Forces and say, "Hi, I'm in need. I'd like to participate in some [Space Forces] activities." Obviously, you'll have to have more restrictions on who can be in the military.

So we imagine most people in any need will likely turn to education. And we'll provide them with their needs, whether it be shelter or food, anything like that. The trade-off will be that you're only eligible to receive this if you're participating in some consumption of education and helping other people around you.

Lastly, we have the US Postal Service. It's a big, moderately skilled workforce. Where do they fit into this? We can't simply say to the post office that anyone who comes asking for a safety net should be given what they need. That would be ridiculous.

But what we can say is that we want to start making some changes. Not drastic changes—just changes that benefit our society. What won't change, of course, is that if people choose to work in the postal system as their full-time vocation, that's great. Keep it up, keep coming to work and doing a great job and getting paid. We love you.

But we're also going to be coordinating with the schools, which now have a lot of people who are obligated to provide some labor to receive their schooling and safety net benefits.

So if you need help and don't want to join the military, ask the school or ask the post office. The post office will tell you to enroll in school, go through that process, and then return.

The school does what they do, figures out what level of classes you should take, what skills you have, and so on. Then, they can refer you to the post office for your part-time minimum-labor obligation. Your labor, then, is helping at the post office. Not necessarily a full-time job, which you are welcome to apply for if you want, but remember what this is. It's a system where people get their needs met by schooling and contributing labor.

At this point, it may seem like communism is being stirred in, as in, we're all helping one another out. And I don't mean helping one another full time. I would imagine there will be a balance that will strike, but if you are a person who's in need of food, shelter, clothing, and so on, for yourself and your family, and you come to a school and say, "Please help me," then they start the process of taking care of you, finding where you can pitch in, and enrolling you in a class. And obviously, you would then find classes based on your current level of accomplishment or education, right? If you need to learn English, they'll teach you that. If you have a college degree, they'll consider that, and you'll start taking classes at that level.

Phil

Stop for a second and think about what happens right there. I have an image in my mind like fish scales. One overlapping another.

For instance, we roll out American Laborism and we say, "Let's start it July 1 of this year." July 1 comes, and one person—we'll call him Bob—shows up to the American Laborism Advancement Department and says, "I understand if I need help, I need to ask you."

Whoever is working at the Advancement Department then helps Bob get enrolled in a days' worth of classes, finds somewhere Bob can work, and arranges for a place for Bob to live and to have some food.

We have to assume for Bob's sake that at least one job, one meal, one class, and some kind of shelter are available.

The next day, maybe Alice and Carlos show up, asking for help. If we're doing this right, everyone is gaining some education that's appropriate to them. And now we have three people we need to feed and shelter, but we also have three people ready to pitch in with some labor.

But America doesn't have three people who need help. America has hundreds of thousands of homeless and millions in poverty, and probably tens of millions who would want to take advantage of free education. They become the fish scales where, on the one hand, each person is both receiving what they need and providing something beneficial to someone else.

And in time, since they're all gaining education, what they can provide for one another is growing as well.

Eric

Nice. And we're not forcing anybody into any kind of rudimentary school. We're customizing this because we'll have people at every level of education and people at every level of need, and we'll help them with that, feed them, and help one another with this. And that is not an oversimplified fairy-tale view of this—that we all join together and hold hands, sing, and help one another. That's not what I mean.

What I mean is that if you ask for help, you will also be providing help. If you are someone who's good with kids, you can help other people by watching their kids. If you're someone who's highly educated, you can help by offering classes, teaching classes, *and everything in between. If we're offering food, then someone's going to have to cook that food, right? So maybe you take one shift, one day out of your week. That's where you dedicate yourself toward helping, policing, cleaning, cooking, anything like that. Whatever skill you have, we'll absorb that and put it to work.*

And, simultaneously, you're being helped and being educated. You're not getting paid, and you're not paying anything into the system for this. There won't be any money changing hands, and anything you need at the very basic level for survival and sustenance, that's what you get.

Nobody's going to get rich off this. And nobody's going to apply for and get double or triple benefits. There is no funny budgeting, corruption, fraud, or kickbacks going to program leaders. There will be no one being given a big budget of money to decide what to hand out and hold back. It is literally just taking care of one another's needs, helping one another, and getting educated. And if you notice, I started by talking about people who need something.

Not everybody needs something.

CHAPTER 8

WHO BENEFITS THE MOST?

AT THIS POINT we have explained how capitalism fails because not everyone has capital. And Marxism fails because some people do have access to capital. We've also explained how labor—especially when coupled with education that increases the value of labor—is a superior foundation for a society.

We've said that American Laborism is better for everyone in America. In this chapter, we'll begin to answer some of the obvious possible rebuttals and put our theory to the test.

Can American Laborism *really* help everyone?

What about people who can't work or people who are very poor? Will American Laborism help them? Conversely, what about rich people? If they don't support American Laborism, perhaps because rich people often don't depend on their own labor as much as people who aren't rich do, will they be against this? And what about very old people? Will American Laborism help them?

Following, we'll work through how people who can't work, poor people, very old people, and even rich people will benefit from American Laborism.

Then we'll take an honest look at a group of people who are very likely to be disrupted the most by American Laborism—maybe as many as millions of people who currently work in the federal government that we are committed to reducing in size. We'll examine how American Laborism helps some of our fellow Americans and might disrupt other friends and neighbors of ours, and then consider if any of this is a price worth paying.

How Can American Laborism Help People Who Can't Work?
Define *work*.

If you look at the definition of work for someone with a highly specialized job, such as a surgeon, astronaut, or professional athlete, then very few people can work the way they work. As we began to explain earlier, work and labor should be seen as a wonderfully wide spectrum of possibilities.

However, to answer the question precisely, let's explore the possibility that someone literally cannot work.

It is important to remember that American Laborism only requires a work contribution from people who request assistance from the federal government. So the question should be, "What about people who need federal help and yet can't work?"

This is important too because it assumes they've exhausted all state, county, city, neighborhood, church, community, and charitable resources and still need assistance.

So for the sake of argument, this is a person who can't work and has no other resources (although we are not convinced such a person even exists). This individual has only three options left: the US Military Department, the US Post Office, and the Advancement Department.

We can't assume this person who can't work would be of no value to the military and unable to serve there. It may not be clear what value they may have, but don't discount the possibility that an aptitude test may uncover something valuable that would be beneficial to the military or even the post office.

But again, for the sake of the question, we'll assume this "can't work" person also has zero aptitude in terms of the military or post office, so they can't seek assistance there.

So the "can't work but needs federal benefits" person should approach any Advancement Department facility or any school, college, or university participating as partners with the Advancement Department and ask for assistance.

They are immediately granted access to nutritious food and

sufficient shelter. They're also scheduled for obligatory meetings with school administrators. (Remember when Phil asked about administrators? Well, here they become crucial to the system working!)

In these meetings, counselors, admissions experts, educators, and administrators will work to find suitable classes or study materials to satisfy the obligatory requirement for everyone seeking assistance to further their education. This is important, too, because if we're expected to accept that someone can't work, it's possible they simply haven't received enough education, training, or certifications, or they face other barriers that increased education can fix.

If this is true, then we can already see the benefits of American Laborism.

Similarly, this "can't work" person is obligated to meet with someone whose role is to find out where this person best fits in with contributing labor.

Now, read this next part carefully, because it's important and part of what makes American Laborism special and sustainable.

The opportunity to contribute labor at this stage is not the same as being hired for a job. This is a small amount of unpaid labor, other than the food, shelter, and educational benefits this "can't work" person is receiving.

So because they aren't receiving any cash or wage compensation, it's important to find anything beneficial for them to work at. In the best case, they would even find their labor efforts enjoyable.

It's also not expected to be full time. Remember, this is contributing a fair amount of labor for the minimum of basic needs being met and advancing themselves. It hardly seems fair to expect someone to work full time and participate in education for merely getting their lowest needs met, so we're not asking that. One day of labor to receive benefits is all you need to contribute.

If this point is still unclear, imagine if someone had bookkeeping skills and somehow also wanted federal assistance. Maybe they wanted to further their education for free. They could likely contribute just one day of labor per week, plus their educational minimums (more on that later), and the rest of their time they are free to do anything they want—including seeking work that pays a cash wage.

Because under the American Laborism system, there is no punishment or garnishment of benefits for someone who also earns income from another source. American Laborism, as a safety net, offers basic minimum support of food, shelter, and education in exchange for a small, fair amount of labor.

But no cash. Therefore, your benefits don't provide for movies, designer handbags, or fancy cars—though you can use some of your extra time to work for them. American Laborism isn't like most "support" or assistance programs under capitalism. In those, if someone works hard and gets paid for it, their benefits are often reduced. There are many reasons for that, and as a society, we may feel it is fair and unfair simultaneously.

However, under American Laborism, it doesn't matter, because benefits aren't cash, and they aren't given to anyone who isn't adding to their education and contributing labor at the same time, so no one would ever begrudge that person from also wanting to work extra. In fact, it's encouraged.

But we've veered into a discussion about people who want to work *extra* and away from someone who can't work *at all*. That's primarily because—as we said—we don't believe there's anyone who has *no value* to offer.

So we task the administrators to uncover that value. Perhaps it takes the form of an entry-level job once held by eager teens . . . sweeping and wiping tables at a restaurant. Or a job millions of brand-new entrepreneurs supported their families on, such as lawn care. Or maybe something less common, such as beta testing websites and applications for errors. It may indeed be a challenge to find an opportunity for this "can't work" person. However, since it's important—as in, American Laborism wants to work for everyone—the administrator will patiently attempt to find suitable work even for people who "can't" work.

If that sounds like a cop-out—"keep trying until you find some"—we would disagree.

Because it's possible this "can't work" individual may be a special case, such as suffering from paralysis, which, according to the Christopher & Dana Reeve Foundation, affects millions of Americans. Therefore, we may have many Americans who, at first glance, appear unable to work.

But by presuming everyone has value to contribute, and by giving educational work advisors the power to keep looking until something suitable is uncovered, no matter how "special case" it may be, we can begin to actually take care of everyone.

Perhaps we're optimistic and idealistic to a fault because we believe the stance of seeing the world full of people capable of contributing value, coupled with the act of relentlessly searching for ways to make that happen, will decrease the number of people thought of as unable to work.

We want everyone to have the option of contributing labor and participating in American Laborism . . . and if we have to work hard to make that happen, we're OK with that.

We'll leave you with a last thought about those folks who, without American Laborism, "can't work." Nearly a century ago, America faced enormous economic hardships and an unprecedented number of jobless people during the Great Depression. President Franklin D. Roosevelt worked with the US Congress to develop programs that used government resources to put people back to work. Out of that, we got the Civilian Conservation Corps (CCC), which paid millions of Americans to work on projects ranging from building dams and infrastructure to clearing trails and campsites in forests. There were other programs besides the CCC, some of which got the nickname "make work" because the purpose was to put people to work, even if the job they got was something the government essentially *made up*.

Whether you agree with FDR's New Deal or not, millions of people benefited from the government when they assumed that having people working was good for our society.

This is, of course, a different time than the Great Depression, and Americans face different challenges than we did in the prior century. But if we give work to everyone who wants it—even those people who are considered unable to work—it will help us in a similar way to how jobs lifted America out of the Great Depression.

Does American Laborism Help Very Poor People?

Here's a peek into another conversation Phil and I had about Laborism, this time about how American Laborism can help the poor.

Phil

Is there a limited number of positions available in a Laborism system? And if there is, how do you determine how to scale to meet everyone's needs?

Eric

In educating, I don't believe so. It can't be limited.

Phil

Who's paying for it? The government?

Eric

Yes. Us. Our taxes. Our taxes pay for it. And its goal is to become a self-sustainable system. We'll have to have people contributing enough to the system so that it can offer education to them—since they're the same people receiving and contributing—if we want to get to 2 percent federal income taxes in the future—hopefully in the not-too-distant future.

Phil

So for now, though, an unlimited amount of funding could be going to this?

Eric

No. Tax revenue will be 10 percent of everything we make, and then eventually dropping to 2 percent and no national debt. Plus, a very small wealth tax.

Phil

What happens when so many people take advantage of this program because they want to obtain a higher education or require some sort of service at a federal level? What's to prevent overwhelming the system? Because America has millions of poor people.

Eric

Well, you can't intellectually say both this isn't going to work and we've got ten million people showing up and asking for this, right?

Phil

How so?

Eric

I'm just thinking logically—if one person shows up and wants to work one day a week but collects full-time benefits, this might not work. Well, it would at least not be self-contained and sustainable.

Phil

So you need a lot of people involved.

Eric

Yes. If ten million people want this—the millions of poor or poverty-level people in America—some aspects will be a challenge at first, but other aspects get easier with scale. Because ten million applicants mean ten million days of labor each week. And if we do this right, that means ten million people share their labor and receive the benefit of ten million people's labor.

Phil

Sounds like if you can get past the initial onboarding—the ramp up—everything works out fine in the long run.

Eric

That's why the system must be self-sustainable. We're not handing out money to people, and we could take advantage of distance learning or virtual learning, and so on. Some of it can be in-class. Everybody learns in different ways, right? Some people need to be in class, and some skills need to be trained face-to-face, I believe. But other skills can be taught digitally.

And the wonderful thing about digital education is that many people can consume it, right? There's no limit to it. Once we find the best way to teach a new person about our civics system, or entry-level, job-type skills, we can replicate that over and over again. And those ten million people are taking care of ten million people—of course, with the benefit of billions of dollars of taxes keeping it all working.

Phil

I guess what we'd be afraid of is what if there's a glut, right?

What if everyone living in poverty in America signs up for this so quickly that there's a shock to the system that it takes some time to get used to?

Eric

You're asking how do we work through all this?

Phil

I mean, they might have nowhere else to turn besides this program, correct? But ten million people at once. . . .

Eric

We can ease our way into it like a ramping-up period. The logistics can be worked out, but I imagine having a first come, first served sign-up, so that the people most interested get onboarded first because they signed up first. And we migrate people over as fast as possible. Without knowing how many partner schools we'll have, let's imagine that to actually make this work, we need—for lack of a better word—facilities that can teach, house, and feed people. Not ten million . . . maybe just a million to start. We can launch when we've built the ability to help a million people, and then grow every week from there by partnering with schools with facilities or building our own.

Phil

What would it take to launch, fully capable of helping everyone?

Eric

All forty million or so people in poverty in America?

Phil

First off, that's a mind-blowing number. And yes. Is it possible?

No ramp-up. No first come, first served—can we help nearly forty million people on day one get out of poverty?

Eric

Do you want to work through it?

Phil

I do.

> *How would you do it? Dream scenario—everything goes the way it's supposed to. What's the plan?*

Eric

First, partner with ID.me or an organization like it to help us sign people up. Second, partner with the Red Cross and every charitable organization, and ask them how they'd feed forty million people three meals a day for a week, and then ongoing. Have the military ready to help with logistics, and their partners that manufacture MREs (meals ready to eat for the military) can gear up for a new customer. The first week of educational advancement—to process forty million people—will have to be virtual for most of them. A day's worth of lessons and placement tests designed to give us an idea of where everyone stands. There's a number of online schools that can develop that.

Phil

That leaves housing and putting forty million people to work for one day.

Eric

Meals and housing don't scale like virtual classes, and of those two, housing is worse. The only possible day-one answer for housing everyone is that they stay in the housing they're already in.

Phil

What about the five or six hundred thousand who are homeless?

Eric

This one will have to ramp up, and the most likely answer is military or disaster relief tents at first. I actually wanted to talk more about that later, so let's do that. And for participating in labor, to launch with the capability to help everyone at once—it may be a bumpy ride at first—divide our forty million by seven, and each day of the week we have 5.7 million people to put to work. Week one, they'll be on the front line in making this work. Help distribute meals. Help clean up after distributing meals. Help other people enroll. Help organize people. Find out what's not working—what bottlenecks we're hitting—and help solve them, or at least report them. Maybe for launch week, we double-dip with the charitable organizations that help feed people—tell them to be ready for millions of "volunteers" who aren't volunteering as much as fulfilling their obligation.

Phil

[Laughs] *It sounds like a circus, but less of a circus than you'd think it would be. It actually sounds possible . . . in a "minimum viable" sort of way.*

Eric

Can you imagine what day 365 will look like compared to day one?

Phil

So we believe we can launch helping everyone who might sign up. What would be a negative? What might keep this from having everyone wanting it?

Eric

For some people, it will be that our safety net is no longer cash. Just the safety net. The safety net of, if you need to eat, we should give you food, right? We shouldn't give you cash.

Phil

Are you saying we can't trust people with their money at a fundamental level?

Eric

No. I'm saying I don't trust the governments, agencies, systems that are cash-focused and not solving the problems. But it is true that some people receive money and they'll buy food and pay their bills—and some people do not. I'm saying that was a lesson that was difficult to impress upon me when I studied economics, because it took me a while to think, Why do we give people cash? If you just give people cash, they'll go out and find what they want. And if someone is willing to live off a one-dollar taco and spend the rest of their thousand dollars of aid on cigarettes and alcohol, then that cigarette and alcohol consumption works its way through the economy, right? I'm going to have to sell them the cigarettes and brew the alcohol, and so on. So there are many deeper arguments from it than that.

But with Laborism, if we're going to treat everyone fairly and get rid of any kind of fraud and misappropriation or misdirection, and so on, because the lore of the administrators making a good living off the government is the other side of the coin of these government programs taking a trillion dollars and then paying out a few billion dollars in benefits. And maybe they pay people who don't need it, right?

American Laborism is the only plan America has ever had that is also aligned with our real desires: take care of people; give them what they need.

Another advantage is that this system offers a perfect balance between a safety net that's temporary and one that's lifelong. And we probably have examples of both in our society, right? People who came into the safety net expecting it to be more temporary than it is, and people who have participated in the safety net longer. And I also feel that it's not fair to them that our society or certain elements of our society have begun to resent someone who participates in the safety net system for a long time.

Personally, I'd like to move our society away from resenting people who need help perpetually, because I don't think that's fair to anybody. I don't think it's fair to the people who need help, and I don't think it's fair to the people who resent them. I think that's an emotional burden we should strip away from one another.

Let's take the example of someone who is on public assistance for an extended amount of time. We'd be lying to think that there aren't people in our society who begrudge and resent them for that, and maybe even feel negatively toward or even look down upon them.

Phil
Especially if they're not providing any kind of what we consider worthwhile service to the community or anyone, right? If they're just living off the system.

Eric
You just worked out the campaign to make Laborism palatable right there. You can't begrudge someone for participating in the safety net of society if they're also giving back into the safety net of society, right? We've allowed that vaunted class of administrators, and yes, I'm speaking to all the people who are afraid they're going to lose their jobs if we shrink the government. With your cushy

jobs, you've worked your way into participating in a society where many of us believe you're letting people stay poor. And I would imagine there are probably many people out there who would find it more palatable to receive assistance if they could give something back, right? In fact, I bet there are people receiving benefits right now who would happily pitch in and help other people, but they've never even been asked. How much valuable American labor is America just ignoring?

The nearly forty million people in America who are either poor or living in poverty is inarguable evidence supporting our contention that "Capitalism Has Failed a Capitalist Nation." How so? Just having poor people in the country doesn't indict capitalism; there are scores of reasons that someone may be poor, and they aren't all related to whether they participate in a capital-based economic system, right?

Well, no. Because America's Gross Domestic Product (GDP), which is defined as the total market value of all goods and services produced in a country—literally how much America "makes"—is either at or near the highest it's ever been. And America's GDP is higher than any other country on the globe. That means America has never "capitalism-ed" more in our history, and yet, we still have people living in poverty.

We have poor people in our rich country.

America's so-called poor people are made up of a broad group who likely have a near-infinite variety of characteristics, experiences, and situations.

The good news is that American Laborism will help all of them. All of them, that is, who *want* to be helped.

The bad news is that their taxes might increase. That's not because we want to balance the budget on the backs of poor people (but we can already predict that's what the marketing department assigned to attack American Laborism will say). No, we're charging taxes to poor people because everyone is equal.

To mandate that everyone must be treated equally, you must be willing to treat them as equals. Laborism believes everyone is equal. It is wrong to say that people with different incomes are not equal, but that is exactly what progressive tax policies do.

Now, let's go back to trying to come up with a suitable understanding of who poor people are.

They are the most important part of American Laborism.

They are the homeless and unemployed as much as they are people working three jobs to pay for rent in a metro area.

They are students struggling to stay on scholarship as much as they are artists who have yet to make money on their work.

They are craftsmen during an economic downturn, when there is no work, and they are service industry people who are fully employed yet unable to keep up with their bills.

They are single and trying to make it on their own, and they are families struggling to take care of each other.

They are entrepreneurs who are working to launch a new business or product, and they are high school dropouts looking for a direction.

They may have valuable skills, or they may be untrained. They may be depressed or hopeful. They may be tired of working or excited to grow and take on new challenges.

American Laborism is beneficial for all of them, and—aside from the fact that hardly anyone likes paying taxes—the "poor" stand to gain a lot from American Laborism, but it's not a handout.

Here's an anecdote that for millions of people is a true story: receiving help or aid can, for some, be a lifesaving necessity—but it can also feel like a stigma or burden. It's sad but true that millions of people who receive help from their church, community, or government do so out of necessity and at the same time begin to feel negatively toward themselves for needing help.

American Laborism removes that entirely, because to participate in any safety-net programs, the recipient will both have to pitch
in to the community with a fair amount of their labor and also participate in education. This alone removes any stigma from receiving assistance, because it's in no way a freebie or handout. Anyone who previously felt negatively about what they were receiving now knows they
are earning it and contributing a fair amount back into the system.

Similarly, once we roll out American Laborism's safety net and
make it available to literally anyone who wants it, we expect America
will have to confront a painful revelation: America will almost
certainly still have some homeless people, even after we implement a
plan that can literally lift 100 percent of any homeless or unhoused
or inadequately housed person out of their situation. We won't truly
know until it happens, but we have to be honest and say that we
expect some insufficiently housed people won't want to change.

Don't make the mistake of reading that as our saying that all
homeless persons are the same. We're not saying that. We *are* saying
to expect to see some folks who opt out of the benefits. Perhaps it
will be because they don't want to contribute a day of labor. Or live
within the standards of the housing provided by either the military
or education facilities. Or sign up for classes. Perhaps the tragedy of
a mental healthcare affliction or drug addiction keeps them from
wanting to opt in.

Of course, we want to see these people helped. And, thankfully, by creating a safety net that can help people who want it, those
trying to help the homeless can focus on the folks who don't take us
up on food, shelter, and education available to them.

Speaking literally and pragmatically, now—and this could get
blunt—America has nearly six hundred thousand homeless people
(see endhomelessness.org). The National Library of Medicine says
"alcohol and drug abuse affects a third of homeless persons."[12] And

AddictionCenter.com says 33 percent of homeless people battle mental illness.[13] Most studies agree that substance and alcohol abuse overlaps with mental illness, so it's impossible to know how many people are affected. But the least it could be would still count hundreds of thousands of homeless people who may opt out due to addiction or because their mental illness struggles prevent them from seeking training and labor contribution in exchange for food and shelter. Whatever the number, if American Laborism can lift everyone else out of homelessness, the state and local programs in place to deal with the remaining harder cases should benefit from more easily identifying and reaching them.

The American Poor Aren't Just the Homeless

But as for the folks—be they homeless or low income or struggling to make ends meet—who do opt in to receive benefits, these so-called poor people will love American Laborism. They are who it was built for.

It's crucial to understand that our society has conducted uncountable amounts of research, analysis, and theorizing, and has taken action in attempts to solve the problem of poverty and homelessness.

In fact, the United States Interagency Council on Homelessness[14] and the US Department of Health and Human Services[15] have a wealth of information on the subject, showcasing their research and putting their huge budget to work in an attempt to reduce homelessness. Keep all that in mind the next time you see a homeless encampment in your town.

Truth be told, this book does not intend to rehash failed attempts, no matter how sincere or expensive they have been.

America spends an estimated $350 billion, or 3.5 percent of the entire economic output of the country, as measured by GDP (Gross Domestic Product) [16] every year, to solve poverty and homelessness.

Worse yet, statistics show that not only are the programs not solving the problem, but also that homelessness and poverty are very close to where they were in the 1970s—so we're spending money and making no progress.

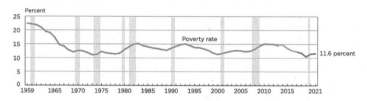

Figure 1. Poverty rate since the 1950s.
https://www.census.gov/content/dam/Census/library/
visualizations/2022/demo/p60-277/figure1.pdf.

The most generous conclusion we could make would be that homelessness and extreme poverty would be worse if we hadn't thrown so much tax money and government at it.

That's admittedly hard to believe, because most of us can't escape the feeling that high taxes and massive bureaucracies aren't the solution when we see the growing number of tents on our streets.

Regardless of whether you're in the "we need to do more" crowd or of a mind that the "more" we're already doing is failing, Laborism solves involuntary homelessness and extreme poverty by throwing the entire power of the federal government at it . . . *efficiently.*

Think about it—whether you look at the current existence of poverty in America after decades of programs and trillions of dollars spent on them as "America has failed Americans" on the one hand or "poverty could have been so much worse" on the other hand, we've made no progress, and it's therefore impossible to argue that had we been implementing Laborism for decades, it would be impossible to see a population with decades more education as anything but progress.

Everyone and anyone who needs food, shelter, or clothing has but to ask for help, and they will receive what they need.

Yes, it's that simple.

By declaring homelessness and poverty a dangerous enemy of America, we will immediately marshal the entire armed services to mobilize against it. (If you're worried about the Posse Comitatus Act, don't be. We cover that in chapter 10.)

We won't describe every detail here, but our military can assemble suitable housing, field hospitals, and facilities for feeding and clothing people.

They'll coordinate with the schools, colleges, and universities to share the opportunity to help people, enroll them in classes, and assign work to them to contribute.

But we can't just stop trying to help. Many of us believe we have a moral obligation to try to bring the poorest of our fellow citizens up to a better life.

And yes, we're well aware that certain poor or homeless people may simply refuse to participate in American Laborism's safety net. For whatever reason they make this choice, that's perfectly fine. American Laborism respects the freedom and will of the individual.

There are no shortage of assumptions and generalizations, either: the homeless are all drug addicts . . . the homeless have mental illness . . . the poor are terrible at managing their time or resources . . . they're uneducated . . . they make terrible decisions . . . they don't want help.

Throw all that out.

Instead, imagine an American person—we'll call her Ms. Monica Smith—is approached by another American person named Robert Jones, and Mr. Jones asks Ms. Smith how he can receive food and shelter because Ms. Smith handles new applications for benefits for a school.

Ms. Smith works with Mr. Jones to provide what he needs—and

what he'll need to do. Within minutes, Mr. Jones—a *person,* not a *story*—can begin to take care of his own needs by trading labor and receiving education. Ms. Smith isn't handing anything out to Mr. Jones or any of the other dozens of people she helps every day.

She's helping America help Americans.

And those who do not come to love American Laborism? They can completely opt out.

Now, what about the cheaters? Those whom we have heard the stories about working the system? That can't happen under American Laborism because no cash benefits are paid.

Naturally, the eradication of cash benefits will upset people, and it won't be just the folks—if there are any—who make a good living collecting cash benefits for what is supposed to be a safety net. In fact, we expect bureaucrats and administrators who are used to controlling huge pools of money and bloated offices full of people who are spending that money will also be upset.

This is the definition of America vs. Americans. Americans pay tax money with the understanding that their money will be used wisely. Yet here we are discussing the possibility that unelected officials can get their hands on the money before it makes its way to help anyone.

The amount of waste in our government is legendary and is covered in depth each year by the nonprofit watchdog organization, Citizens Against Government Waste.

But let's be positive about this by thinking long-term. We believe the increase in paying taxes among poor people will be an acceptable trade-off for receiving dignified assistance that they earn by their labor contributions and unlimited education. The assistance that has been promised to them will finally arrive.

Poor people who want to improve themselves, then, will love American Laborism.

What about Very Old People? How Do They Fit In?

Perhaps you've read this far, and your question is whether older people will also be required to contribute labor and pursue education.

One of the best things about American Laborism is that the system does not discriminate against anyone. It is a system designed for the sole purpose of helping those who need help. There will always be positions readily available for individuals of all ages. But it's important to remember that retirement and enjoying one's later years is still an option. No one is being forced into a position of labor. In fact, it's quite the opposite, as American Laborism only requires labor and education participation from people looking for federal safety net benefits.

With that said . . . yes, if an elderly person wants benefits, the rules also apply to them.

It is not uncommon for the elderly to regret retiring too early. They are typically looking for opportunities to not only stay busy and mentally sharp but also to give back to their community.

A common misconception today is that the very old members of society are somehow unable to adequately contribute to the labor market to perform tasks that "should" be delegated to a younger generation of workforce employees. Not only is this an ageist mentality, it is also simply wrong.

There is a massive pool of skilled labor positions to be provided at any age, and outlining these opportunities would be required at the federal level.

Old age shouldn't stop people from learning new skills or working. A new safety-net system that requires work and education from elderly people would have many positive benefits. In addition to the benefits already mentioned, continuing education can also give individuals a sense of personal growth and a way to stay engaged in the world around them. The new system would help keep elderly people active and involved by providing them with tasks that would challenge and engage their minds and bodies. So let's not be afraid of this change, but instead empower older adults to continue learning and growing, while also contributing to society in a meaningful way.

But perhaps you're worried about the actuality of older people working, or you are struggling with the idea of someone approaching the end of their life pursuing further education.

Let's talk about working first. Of course, it's possible that there are some jobs an older person physically couldn't do. It may be a challenge, at first, to find the best fit for everyone. However, the severity of what we face should motivate everyone in our society to try to find a solution.

If we only need to help a few people, without even diving into it too deeply, we can imagine it won't be a big challenge. Thinking beyond the obvious cliche of having older workers greet shoppers (hat tip to Walmart; I like being greeted by a human being when I enter a store!), we can imagine a wide variety of roles for people with experience, management skills, patience, and unending talents that have served them well for decades.

As for continuing their education, we believe in our system. At its foundation, American Laborism knows that individuals gain value from furthering their education. Some people who are more pragmatic or less optimistic may think it is a waste of time and resources to educate someone in their later years.

We'll go deeper into this subject when we contemplate how people who never want to leave school might fit in with American Laborism, but for now we'll say that we believe that even the oldest people in society can benefit from adding to their education.

Some folks might study subjects they're already deeply familiar with to gain an even greater understanding. Others may want to learn completely new things.

Some people may take any class and do any job offered to them, just so they can take advantage of the American Laborism safety net. We welcome them all, and for that last group, we're happy we can help them live a dignified, productive life. Especially when you consider that Social Security may not provide enough benefits; inflation robs people of their purchasing power. To get benefits, you only need a day of school and a day of work each week.

Will Rich People Get Anything Out of American Laborism?

We think rich people should love this concept, as it benefits the country they live in, improves the lives of their fellow citizens, and lowers the taxes they pay. Maybe they won't be filing for benefits, attending classes, and contributing a day's work each week, but they will indeed benefit from American Laborism.

Unfortunately, we're about to see the real effects of political marketing, which is a type of marketing that somehow convinces people to work against their own interests.

In fact, that is precisely how we find ourselves in the position that America often doesn't act in the best interests of Americans! Our country convincing us to work against ourselves is the very definition of "America vs. Americans"!

That probably sounds more cynical than we truly are, and we hope we're wrong, but only time will tell. Here's what that means:

In this book, we're sharing a very specific economic system with numerous benefits. But big changes will need to be made. And here is where the marketing starts.

Expect to see even people who would benefit from American Laborism start to question whether this is a good idea.

No doubt you'll hear that it's impossible to implement, even from people who up until the second before American Laborism was presented advocated for more free education (such as the most progressive politicians). They will immediately be subjected to marketing that will attempt to turn the dialogue to "We want free education, but not if we have to lower taxes to get it!"

That's just one argument we anticipate. But it's not hard to see the possibility of finding aspects of American Laborism that can be used to pit people against what they know would be superior. Imagine if you weren't reading this book, but instead you were just being fed pieces of it, such as "Poor people will pay as much in taxes as rich people!" or that we're giving free education to everyone, without hearing the intelligent reasoning behind American Laborism. With enough political marketing, you could probably convince people to vote against making America better, right?

On a more positive note, though, Americans who resist the divisive marketing, including rich and wealthy people, will love American Laborism if they came about their riches in any legitimate fashion—probably 95 percent of the rich.

That 5 percent who either cheated, corrupted, bribed, skimmed, or somehow became rich by illegitimate means may not like it as much. They may even fight this like their lives depend on it.

We're not going to spend too much time being negative, but imagine someone has concocted the perfect scheme to overcharge the government, and it's made them rich. We're aiming to eliminate that. And frankly, taking them on may be another big hurdle American Laborism faces.

Thankfully, the vast majority of rich people came about their wealth legitimately. Remember, America is a capitalist society, and there are many ways to become wealthy.

We believe they're going to love this.

In fact, you should know that while we aim for American Laborism to solve problems for all Americans and lift the poorest to where their labor earns them more, we'd consider American Laborism a success if wealthy and ultra-wealthy people from around the world moved to America to take advantage of a fair tax system and general improvement of everyone's standard of living.

So yes, rich people will love this. First, their tax bill to the federal government will plunge. Don't be fooled by clever anecdotes about rich people not paying any taxes. American Internal Revenue Service statistics show America's current income tax rules charge the rich the highest taxes, thanks to one of the most progressive tax systems in the world.[17]

You've likely seen the charts that show that people who earn more than the $69,000 US median household income, as reported by the 2020 census, pay 92 percent of all income taxes the IRS collects. It's pretty clear that the American rich pay a lot in taxes.

After rolling out a fair tax for everyone, expect there to be a period when society must retrain themselves to operate under such a system. It's no small feat to break away from a progressive tax. Admittedly, there is something that feels fair about taking a proportionally higher amount of the income or wealth from a successful person—even if it is exactly the opposite of fair.

And whether you're rich or not, you can agree that only the most courageous of rich and wealthy people will speak out in favor of a fair flat tax. America has trained itself to think we want more from people who have more (a staple of Marxism we now cling to as if we need to be absurdly unfair and discriminatory toward people).

And, we suspect, this is also why so many people believe there are loopholes and strategies that rich people use to avoid paying taxes. Perhaps there is some truth to that. It makes sense that the community as a whole may believe that levying punishing taxes on the wealthy is a good idea, while individuals may seek to relieve themselves of the high tax burden they themselves voted for!

But common sense tells us that punishing successful people isn't a good long-term strategy.

Moreover, we have only to look at the actual yearly collected tax revenue of our country—which is at or near an all-time high of $4.71 trillion[18]—and compare that to our national debt of nearly $33 trillion to know that we've failed.

But this is where it's the easiest to see how America vs. Americans plays out. If we are indeed paying record amounts in taxes and simultaneously accumulating unprecedented levels of debt, shouldn't we expect to receive the best governmental services possible and have unprecedented levels of investments in the future, and every problem our government faces be solved?

Debt isn't a bad strategy if it's used to create value. But finding that value as a result of the debts we currently owe is impossible. America has taken money from Americans both present and future and delivered very little value for it.

So back to the rich people we're certain we'll be pleasing with American Laborism.

Let's imagine rich people fall somewhere between perfectly selfish and perfectly altruistic. Selfish people might think that lowering their taxes and making everyone equal appeals to them. If they own a business, it may also appeal to them that the work-force they rely on is participating in free, unlimited training and education, and therefore the collective ability of the labor pool is constantly increasing. Competing businesses in other countries won't stand a chance against an American labor force that has free access to unlimited education.

But if they're rich and care only about other folks generously and altruistically, they'll appreciate that Laborism now provides a better, robust safety net for the entire country. And beyond the best safety net ever created will be opportunities to succeed!

So, not considering people who are rich from fraud or are skirting their tax responsibilities, it's easy to see how rich people will appreciate all that Laborism has to offer.

What Happens to Teachers?

You might be wondering what happens to teachers, educators, professors, and anyone in the teaching profession if we're closing the Department of Education and creating the Advancement Department. Won't there be lots of teachers out of work?

Don't worry, closing the Department of Education won't put many teachers out of a job, because the department employs very few teachers with the $88.3 billion they requested for 2023.

Rather, most teachers work for cities, counties, and states, and are paid by such.

But because the Advancement Department will be taking on the role of educating anyone who wants it (a role the Department of Education doesn't currently have), we'll actually be *hiring* huge numbers of teachers.

Will teachers be put out of work? No. They'll have even more options for where they can work and lots of jobs available to them.

What Happens to People Who Work for the Federal Government?

While we believe converting America from a capital-based to a labor-based society has long-term permanent advantages that solves numerous problems for our population—including more than we've covered so far (but will be covering later)—American Laborism isn't proposing changing *only* our focus on the value of labor; there are other noteworthy changes as well.

Remember, a big part of what we are proposing is to dramatically shrink the size and responsibilities of the executive branch of our federal government. That will also yield numerous benefits. Our taxes will decrease. Our government will be more efficient and focused on the needs of Americans and more responsive to those needs. Our budget deficit and our national debt can finally start the long journey to financial solvency for America.

However, there is no avoiding the fact that reducing the size of the federal government, which has become the biggest employer in America, is likely to cause significant disruption in the lives of many government employees.

This is a necessary part of the progress we want to see, but that makes it no less challenging to work through. We want to share with you the conversation we had on the subject, so you can see our thought process while working to accept the paradox of putting people out of work to make Laborism possible.

Eric

One of the biggest employers in the country is our federal government, right?

Phil

Right, the federal government has reach into nearly every aspect of our lives, and in doing so, manpower is required.

And sure, there are probably thousands of people working in the government now who are keeping programs alive, helping, and sincerely following what is best for people.

But there are other people who work just to get a paycheck both in the private sector and for the government. They may not even be helping anything at all. We may not like this, but we're going to have to deal with millions of them losing their jobs if we drastically reduce the size of government.

So how are you going to convince those people? Especially if you're going to take away government power, and where's that power going exactly?

Eric

Anything that the federal government is doing now, other than taking care of people's basic needs, providing military, educational advancement, and postal services can be rolled down to the states or absorbed by those three surviving executive branch departments or the private sector.

Phil

So what are we doing with federal government jobs? There are millions of people employed by the federal government right now.

Eric

We have to start with a hiring freeze; then some are going to be eliminated due to attrition as their departments are shrunk, and some will indeed be displaced.

Phil

Where do those people go?

Eric

They go back out into the free market. Back into the workforce or into the military or post office or into the school system . . . like all Americans.

Phil

So they're going to go from a government-paid job with significant benefits into the private sector that doesn't provide the same benefits?

Eric

That's one choice. Or another choice is they can take their skills out into the marketplace.

Phil

It sounds like a lot of them will become unemployed.

Eric

If someone who is displaced by the reduction of the size of the federal government just absolutely doesn't fit into the military, post office, or advancement areas, but they are only willing to work in government, then they can look for positions at the state, county, city, or other municipality level.

Phil

What if there aren't enough jobs, enough work, and enough to be done at those levels? What if there are simply more people displaced than all replacement government positions combined?

Eric

We seem to be really dancing around the concept that our government, the largest employer in America, may have too many employees. If that's true, are American taxpayers really obliged to overstaff their government when we're running a nearly $2 trillion annual deficit? Maybe the solution for government workers who only like to work for the government is the tough medicine that we don't need as many as we have.

And we certainly don't need people, by the nature of who employs them, having some kind of special status. We can't have a "government class" of protected workers at their taxpaying neighbors' expense. That's not fair for society for us to want to keep that going. It's unsustainable.

And it may be such that some of those people do have to adjust. That's the price we're going to have to pay to shift from a system that's not working and that most people believe is unfair.

But let's look at taxes and the services they buy us a different way. If you have a medical service that you think your neighbors should be paying for, would you walk around and ask them for that? We don't do that, do we? But they are the ones paying.

Let's apply the same thing for the job a government employee does. If someone has a job providing services for your neighbors, would you feel comfortable walking around and presenting your work product—your quarterly update—to your neighbors and asking them to pay you directly? Because that's exactly what the government is doing.

Phil

I would still imagine there would be serious backlash from many federal workers who don't want to be put out of work. How is American Laborism going to appeal to them?

Eric

Would they expect to keep their jobs if our debt spiraled uncontrollably out of hand—such that just making the interest payments requires us to start cutting programs that we can no longer afford, taking us to where this American Laborism system looks better than that bankrupting American alternative?

On the other hand, another possibility is that we could get a leader in, or a series of leaders, who ran the government more like a business. People say all the time that they wish the government was as efficient as a business—although you don't hear the bureaucrats who are living off of it saying that as often.

Imagine we got a leader who ran the government like a business and was able to pare it down and let people retire out. If nothing else, we could begin passing laws that bridge our way over to American Laborism not replacing anybody who retires out of a position that is not either military or advancement. We'd simply not replace them. And every other job is going to be shifting over to education and the military. And if it's one at a time, it's one at a time. And if you think about it, this is the same problem and solution.

Phil

What does that mean? A slow transition, allowing current federal workers to retire out of the current system?

Eric

Either this is a small problem, and we have a small number of administrators who won't be able to find their way in this new system, or we have a big number of those people, right? I'm fairly certain there's something like three million federal employees currently, but that doesn't tell us how many of them would be displaced. If the number we don't need to hold over is big, like in the millions . . . well, that's the problem that got us here.

To answer your question in what's probably going to sound brutal: if they absolutely cannot find themselves in this system then they'll find themselves on the receiving end of this system. And we can soften it as much as possible. We can transition over a year at a time, or something like that, if society looks at this and says it's worth doing, and it's a goal I'd like to get to. For those millions of people that are working for the federal government and not producing very much, society does need to offramp them slowly. But I believe that this system is worth implementing faster than that because I think we're in too deep right now.

Phil

Plus, it may be disruptive, but if American Laborism is to be fair, equal, and include no discrimination, then a disrupted federal employee can be treated the same as a disrupted welder, teacher, bookkeeper, manager, or entrepreneur, right?

Eric

Yes, they can.

What Happens When We Disrupt
American Government Employment?

We have discussed attrition as one way to reduce the number of federal employees, with some being absorbed into remaining departments. Now let's talk about the plan and explore other options.

The plan to transition to American Laborism is simple. First, implement a hiring freeze in the federal executive branch to passively reduce government size. Second, evaluate departments that are approaching their sunset to determine which functions are critical to America's safety and prosperity and which ones are bloated bureaucracy. The critical functions should continue operating under the military, advancement, post office, or a combination.

Next, reduce staff by either letting them go or repositioning them elsewhere. Effective employees can seek opportunities in the Advancement Department, which begins with no employees. Others can be retrained for the private sector or opt for retirement.

While private labs and researchers can still collaborate with the government, the provision of services by the federal government should go through one of the designated channels. For instance, the critical functions of the Department of Energy can be absorbed into a combination of military and education, working together to leverage the highest technology possible.

Now let's address the question of what the federal government desires the most. Tax money, of course. However, more tax money inevitably leads to more power for the government. Power translates to control, and the government thrives on being in control. Individuals' dependence on the system benefits the government, and the bloated departments trying to justify their own existence.

When discussing the bureaucratic class, we acknowledge that some individuals may have saved money over the years and can take care of themselves. If you have been living well as a bureaucrat or government employee and have no retirement or savings, you may be affected by these changes. However, trained individuals with degrees and experience in administration may have valuable skills to offer and could be compensated accordingly if they choose to explore opportunities outside the government.

Right now in America, more than one in ten people are living in poverty according to the most recent census. That's nearly forty million people who need help and can be helped, lifted out of poverty, thanks to American Laborism.

If we have to run the risk of disrupting the employment of a few million federal employees to solve poverty in America, that's a price worth bearing. Especially considering advances in AI are expected to disrupt up to 47 percent of the white-collar workforce (nearly half of America), thereby disrupting many tens of millions of people who could be retrained and return to the workforce, making advancements if we have American Laborism, or they could struggle with government inefficiency if we don't.

CHAPTER 9

REMAKING THE EDUCATION SYSTEM

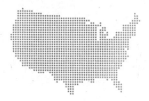

Phil

In terms of training or education, do you think schools will take on more students than what they are now? A lot more?

Eric

Yes, they will. Well, the federal government will now welcome everybody at any age and education level who wants to advance their education. And anyone who needs help . . . also welcome. Schools will be busy.

Think of this as having a double-wide front door—wide enough to let people in who need help and who want to improve their labor or just get educated. Either way, they're taken care of.

Phil

What happens if they don't leave? If they just want to learn for the sake of learning. They don't want to work. They just do their classes, work a day each week, and never want to leave.

Eric

That's OK. It's actually great. That's somebody I wouldn't begrudge whatsoever, because we're also going to match the curriculum to their ability. They'll be contributing, so that could become valuable over time to everyone around them if they've been in school for decades, right?

Won't Some People Want to Stay in School Forever?

We understand that asking a question like this is an attempt to critique American Laborism, as if pursuit of perpetual education is some sort of underhanded loophole being taken advantage of.

Hardly! We sincerely hope people will want to do this.

As both a country and as neighbors, we should want what is best for our society, and that includes giving people who want to get an education the opportunity to do so.

Don't forget that the "free, unlimited" education comes with strings attached, and the receiver has to share some of their labor.

Think of this as a fair trade-off and let your optimistic imagination run with it, because in this chapter, we're about to undo a lot of what has turned America into working against the interest of Americans.

Imagine our "forever student" continues to seek more education. Eventually you'd expect they'll have acquired some level of competence or even expertise in a subject. In a later chapter, we'll discuss what might happen if they take that expertise and leave school with it. For this chapter, we'll discuss someone who wants to stay in school forever.

They could then share that expertise as part of their labor obligation by teaching others who pursue their education. Imagine how lucky the students of a person who wanted to stay in school forever would be to have that kind of expertise!

Or our forever student may not want to teach but could instead *labor* by writing about what they are learning, such that other people can benefit from their words.

If nothing else, this forever student could work for the school in an overseer or admin or counselor capacity. There is no limit to what someone who genuinely wants to keep learning could offer. As they continue to add to their education, they can become experts on subjects. Thought leaders. Authors. Fact-checkers. Policy advisors. Professors. Entrepreneurs. Consultants.

Let's make up a person and imagine they are the sort who never wants to leave school. We'll call this person Meg. Meg accepts the terms of American Laborism, accepts the housing and meals offered, signs up for classes, and takes whatever work the system offers her. By working one day a week in the system, Meg can stay as long as she takes classes.

We can think of a few possible futures for Meg.

Maybe Meg is happy living this way. In this scenario, Meg keeps taking classes forever and works at least one day a week at whatever job she's assigned . . . forever. It's not hard to see how someone willing to work to keep up their part of the social bargain of American Laborism is perfectly acceptable.

Another possible future for Meg could be that the assigned job doesn't make her happy. So Meg starts asking for work that might match her interests better. She even applies some of what she's learned toward this new job. Meg is still simply working within the system, but her contribution is increasing because she is applying her growing education.

Yet another possible future is that Meg takes her growing body of knowledge and a little bit of her spare time and begins to work beyond the minimum. Maybe it's writing a book. Maybe it's working two days a week. One day's work covers Meg's obligation, and the other day earns her some pay. Meg can travel, buy herself anything she wants, hire other people, or spend her money any way she wants. (And yes, Meg will pay 10 percent income tax on her earnings.) In a nutshell, if Meg wants so much as a pack of cigarettes or to go out for a nice dinner, she'll have to work a little bit beyond the minimum.

Yet another future could see Meg becoming the most educated person ever on whatever subject interests her. Imagine a lifelong learner faced with the possibility that they've become the foremost expert on a subject. We'd like to think Meg then seeks out other experts, consults with them, advances the state of knowledge on the subject, and pushes the body of American knowledge forward. Wouldn't that be amazing?

But perhaps none of that happens. Perhaps Meg just works one day a week—the bare minimum—and then consumes as much education as possible.

Will our society accept that someone might be interested in "working the system" to contribute the minimum and consume the maximum?

This question presupposes that education is valuable, right? We would agree with that! But not in the sense that it should be in any way limited or restricted; rather, we hope we've painted a picture that when we say "free and unlimited education," that should in no way be seen as a cost to society, but rather a benefit to be maximized.

This is a wonderful paradox, isn't it? That education is so valuable that some folks may begrudge people who attempt to consume as much of it as possible from a system that offers it for free.

We'll close this section with one last thought: Meg contributes to society in every scenario, and her basic needs are being met by a combination of her own contributions and the contributions of others, and the very low tax rate of American Laborism. Lifelong students, such as Meg, should be welcomed, and even encouraged, to participate.

Let's consider what we're talking about when we say *education*. Up to this point, we've somewhat assumed that you, the reader, have an idea of what we're talking about. But if the premise of this section is that we welcome people who decide they want to participate in education forever . . . what exactly are we signing up for? What exactly is *education*?

One basic, commonly held understanding of *training* or *education* is simply transferring knowledge and/or skills from a source that has the information to someone who does not.

So when someone "receives education" by participating in

American Laborism, the exact plan would be to supplement whatever knowledge, skills, and traits they already have.

And yes, that means if someone is barely educated or even not at all educated, we'd start at the beginning. We may have to start with language, math, and even basic study skills.

On the other hand, if someone has already received an advanced degree yet wants to further their education, they'd, of course, be able to keep studying to further their already impressive education.

Theoretically, it's possible that someone could achieve such a high level of knowledge and skills in a subject that there could be nothing left for them to learn on the subject. Thankfully, the education provided by American Laborism is unlimited—and here's how we'd accommodate that.

First, it's hard to imagine someone would find themselves in a position where there was literally nothing left to learn in their field of study—but let's assume it's possible. It's also hard to believe that this person holds the ultimate body of knowledge on a subject and does not wish to share their unique perspective by entering the private sector, writing a book, inventing, starting a company, teaching classes, or consulting for other universities. If any of these or similar scenarios attract this person to apply their unique knowledge, they are then benefitting society by giving back what they've learned. They may even make a huge profit on their time or expertise by being such a thorough expert on the subject!

But for the sake of discussion, let's accept that all that person wants to do is keep learning.

Here's where one of American Laborism's superpowers kicks in: freedom of choice. People are welcome to seek education either of what they need to learn or what they want to learn. This is not just the people who have achieved the rare distinction of "knowing everything" on a subject, either. *Anyone* can choose what they want to study.

Of course, just like the education systems that succeed around the world, including our own, we must expect there to be an order that someone has to follow while they are learning. You can't study calculus or accounting if you haven't passed basic math, for example.

But we'll be expecting to teach on any subject from trades to culinary arts to math and sciences to business management, life sciences, and even medicine. As long as someone has met the prerequisites for any class or field of study, they can pursue whatever they like.

Of course, some people will opt for a pragmatic education that can help them achieve more at work or running their own company. Others may not be as focused and opt to study a variety of subjects. In fact, we imagine people may discover hidden talents or fascinations by trying different fields of study. I (Eric) was very interested in studying architecture, for example—until I fell in love with my economics classes!

As for people who intend to stay in school forever and maybe completely avoid working in the private sector, as long as they're contributing their labor to cover their obligation to receive further education, they can keep adding more disciplines to their knowledge base *ad infinitum.*

But please note: we honestly believe that the lure of entrepreneurship, subject matter expert, teaching, or writing will appeal to someone who is highly educated, and they'll want to "cash in" on the education they've received. So the idea of a student never leaving school is interesting—and frankly, a risk we're willing to take—but we think it's more realistic to think people with that much knowledge will want to share it somehow for everyone's benefit.

What about People Who Leave School and Join the Private Sector?

More power to them. We want that to happen!

Laborism is a cradle-to-grave safety net for people who want it. But it's also completely at your discretion. Come and go as you please. In fact, it makes perfect sense that someone who wants to take advantage of their education or increased skills can enter the workforce, start their own business, do anything they want . . . knowing they can return to school whenever they need to.

Laborism is a safety net, not a cage!

Even better, Laborism is a revolving door. If you need to, you are allowed to leave and come back as often as you like, without any negative consequences or having to wait to get your benefits reinstated.

That is how benefits should be designed—options available to those who need them, not a system that creates dependency.

Think about why the image of benefits as a safety net has persevered for so long. It's a great analogy, conjuring up the image of a trapeze artist flying through the air. The safety net doesn't limit how high they can fly; it simply provides a safe place for them to fall. That gives the aerialist *more* confidence to strive to fly *even higher*.

That's what we want for everyone under American Laborism too! Because America—when it isn't working against the interests of its people with inflationary, restrictive, and punitive financial policies—is a land of opportunity, full of chances for those who are willing to work hard. And to be that land of opportunity, we need to ensure that people can learn as much as they want, then take their skills to the private sector, and always be welcomed back for further education and support if they need it. We need to be a country where people can have access to quality education and training throughout their lives. We're creating a society that is truly supporting people with opportunity!

Plus, the private sector benefits by hiring people who, by all expectations, should be educated to the fullest extent possible. You can expect that better-trained people will earn more too.

Simply put, we hope people gain so much education through

our program that they leave and never need benefits again, and prospering whenever they are working or starting their own business.

But the benefits are available for them if they do need them again.

Doesn't that sound like a perfect plan to encourage people to figure out what works best for them, rather than attempt to live within guidelines that may not take into account an individual's needs?

If someone seeks benefits, gains more education (while also contributing labor), and then returns to the workforce with more knowledge, training, skills, or character traits, they should be getting paid more for their labor. And that's exactly what basing our society on labor rather than capital will yield.

Eric

You asked earlier why someone who's already successful in their career would choose to participate in this. That's a fantastic segue over to solving this without money, which means people looking for monetary compensation won't get it from the safety net.

I know economists will fight us on this. They're going to say the safety net needs to be cash, because there are many schools of economics that believe that, and they have convincing arguments for it. But I don't believe it. If this is American Laborism, if what we respect among our fellow humans is their ability to provide work, labor, and help, then if that's what they have to offer to the safety net, we're not going to compensate it with cash. If their labor is worth the cash, take it out into the free market and acquire cash for it.

Phil

Would there be positions that could be compensated for in the federal government?

Eric

Yes, if you are contributing more than just the one day a week of labor to get your benefits. But as we downsize the government, there may not be any unfilled jobs.

Phil

And jobs at the schools would fall under that too?

Eric

Can I answer mostly yes? Yes, they would. If you are working for the school, whether in an office or any other capacity, and you want more work than just the one day per week, they can compensate you. But don't forget, the school is tasked with making sure everyone who needs to contribute labor can do that. So the school will have to work with that.

But let's take this further. When you contribute a day of labor, that's a job. It's part time, but it's a job. Anywhere anyone works, the employer is always on the lookout for talent. How many times will we see someone take a job working just one day a week and then their talent begins to show through, and they start getting paid to work an extra day or more?

As time goes by, maybe they leave school entirely, maybe they gradually move from part-time worker and student to part-time student? Whatever is right for them is what they should do.

As your labor increases in value, you'll have more options.

What Does American Laborism Think about People Who Can Make More Money Working for Themselves?

We say, do it!

Pay federal taxes equal to 10 percent of whatever you make plus 0.25 percent of whatever you own each year, and we'll leave you alone.

Once the federal debt is paid off, send us 2 percent of whatever you make and 0.25 percent of whatever you own once a year, and we'll leave you even "alonier." This section will discuss taxes a fair amount, because if you opt out of receiving benefits, paying your taxes is your only obligation in an American Laborism economy.

But it's a valid question contemplating that once American Laborism is rolled out, what about the people who don't need it? What about people who aren't interested in merely having their needs met? What about people who do just fine without contributing labor and enrolling in school?

We're talking about people who don't need something from society's safety net. We can imagine most people will think, *Hey, I'm fine. I have my own practice, or I like my job, or I'm highly skilled, or I'm a professional athlete, or whatever it is. I don't need anything from this.*

If we haven't made it clear, understand that participating in the American Laborism safety net is voluntary. Most welfare-type safety-net systems are partially voluntary. For instance, if you want to receive SNAP benefits, you must apply for them and qualify to receive them. Likewise with unemployment. We're not trying to confuse the issue, because many of these programs are administered by the state you live in, so it's not a direct analogy to the federal government providing benefits in every case.

But remember, we used the phrase *partially voluntary* because obviously the taxes we pay under our existing systems are not voluntary.

If you're still reading and still think unlimited, free, lifetime education—a safety net that promises to meet all of someone's needs—and a community all helping one another sounds Marxist or communist, the fact that anyone who doesn't want to participate can opt out should dispel that comparison!

But the question, which is the focus of this section, presupposes that people are worried about having to participate in mandatory pursuit of education and contribution of labor. Perhaps different people will be in the group who need benefits over time, and maybe some people will never need benefits. To those people, the answer is, you don't have to participate if you don't want to, other than paying your taxes. The American Laborism system will continue to run with or without any specific individual's participation.

But it's not just well-off or even financially comfortable people who may not want to participate to receive benefits. There could also be poor people who choose not to participate.

When considering individuals who may not require these benefits, some may choose to live independently, regardless of their needs. Some people simply do not wish to be part of a system, regardless of the benefits offered.

And that's perfectly OK. If someone prefers a lifestyle that others may perceive as lacking in housing, education, or healthy eating, they have the option to decline benefits. This is a free country, and individuals have the right to self-determination under American Laborism. If they choose not to participate in or contribute to the system, they are free to live independently.

Let me be clear: this is not meant to sound cruel or dismissive. It means that if someone is self-sufficient and able to live independently to any extent, they have that choice. However, we also expect individuals to adhere to standards of safety, sanitation, and respect for others' property within their respective communities. It is the responsibility of communities to ensure that all residents meet established standards.

But there will also be people who are successful enough who say, "I certainly don't want to live on a maintenance level. I don't want to live at the bare minimum. I don't want to participate in this by cooking for other people, by cleaning, or by taking classes. I'm doing well for myself. I'll stick with what I've got and what I'm doing." And they can, because in this instance, we would be looking at that most people are employed, skilled, fortunate, or independent enough, they can provide for themselves an acceptable life. That's wonderful. We're not going to curtail that in any sense, besides the taxes that everybody has to pay into the system.

I want Laborism to spread around the world, and I want everyone's needs to be met. And I want us to treat one another with fairness and balance. I believe this is the way to do it. I believe that someone who wants to opt out, can. Now, you can opt out of the training and education system, you can opt out of participating by giving your time or taking classes, and you can opt out of military service, but you can't opt out of the taxes. I believe this is a fair amount of taxes, and it helps incentivize our country and society to get out of debt—it's a lot easier to get *into* debt than it is to get *out of* debt. It's unfair over time to strap people with debt that they didn't vote themselves into. My goal would be to pay it all off. That may take a little work, and there are surely people who are not paying taxes now who will bristle at this.

Most people don't realize that half of Americans don't pay any taxes at all. They have no tax burden at the federal level. That's because we've worked our way from a very small tax a century ago (that was supposed to be temporary) into where we are now trying to socially modify the country based on what we think is fair. We think, *That guy makes a lot of money. That girl makes a lot of money. That person is very fortunate. Let's charge them more taxes!*

The federal government should not be in that business whatsoever; it's a form of discrimination because we're treating two people differently based on their income.

There is nothing more capitalist than to think that the capital someone owns makes them different from the person sitting next to them. To move away from capitalism, we'll have to give that up. But the benefit we get is that literally anyone who needs anything can be taken care of, but not by punishing somebody else. We'll meet the needs of everyone, and we'll do it without overcharging by reducing the amount of government we need, especially when that government is inefficient. So the simple part of Laborism—which may have an immediate impact—is introducing the idea to people that Laborism can even exist.

The definition of Laborism needs to be expanded in people's minds so that it isn't just benefits and entitlements. It goes deeper than that and will improve how we all live—even the people who never ask for any help.

What Happens to People with Massive Student Loans?

Thanks to the Department of Education, America has a massive student loan problem. It's such a big problem that, including federal and private loans, the amount has reached $1.6 trillion in total.[19] Over the past thirty years, tuition for public four-year colleges has increased dramatically, and today, more than half of students leave school with debt. This is another example of the American government working against Americans. This time, though, it's our students who are on the receiving end of America vs. Americans. With that said, it's unlikely that a solution exists that will make *everyone* happy.

That's because people who never took out student loans, as well as the people who paid them off themselves, aren't typically in favor of the "just wipe them all clean" solutions politicians typically offer as a vote-getting "solution" for those deeply in debt. Plus, a 2023 US Supreme Court decision struck down President Joe Biden's plan to do just that: wipe away $400 billion of student loan debt.[20]

It hardly seems fair that only some folks pay their student loans or—through taxes or inflation—pay the loans of other people, but it also hardly seems fair that universities pile massive debts on individuals with very little hope of repaying it. You've undoubtedly heard stories about people with tens or hundreds of thousands of dollars of student debt for a degree of questionable worth.

See what we mean? Where is the solution that respects everyone and treats them fairly?

Here's the Laborism take: we're looking for the money in all the wrong places.

It shouldn't surprise you that American Laborism can solve this.

First, America already has many programs that can help people with student loans work toward getting out from under them. Those can stay in place for the people they are suitable for.

Second, we need to reduce the amount being loaned out to keep the huge debt bubble from getting any bigger.

Third, we need to make it clear that there isn't going to be any kind of "debt jubilee" where billions of dollars of loans are just forgiven. Wiping ridiculous loans from one person at the cost of society having to pay it is not fair.

Sadly, some shameless politicians claim young adults can't be trusted with financial decisions and should have done just that for them. But those same politicians don't extend that generosity to the debts incurred by a young entrepreneur starting a new business.

This is hypocrisy.

It should come as no surprise that under American Laborism, the federal government will no longer offer any guarantee, subsidy, or other type of participation in any way with newly created student loans.

Zero.

If you are a lender, you should know that the Advancement Department will not back, guarantee, or otherwise help with any loan going forward. Loans that are already contractual obligations of guarantors will run their course. No new federally guaranteed loans will be issued. The amount of student loans already in existence and tied to the federal government will need to be paid off, not increased.

Even though it might not be popular to demand people pay their own debts, American Laborism will continue to push for this, because one of its goals is to help America get rid of all debt. Requiring America's citizens to assume the responsibility to pay billions or trillions of dollars of other people's student loan debt is going the wrong direction, and it won't happen under American Laborism.

However, it's not all bad news for people carrying huge debts. In addition to the programs already available, the Advancement Department will work with Congress to create new programs that will allow people who are heavily indebted to claim refunds from the money held by the university, college, or school that helped them rack up those debts. Yes, it's time to look toward the beneficiaries of those easy loans and enlist their help. No entity benefited more from easy loans than colleges who collected massive tuition, which was fueled by student debt. We don't expect the schools to be happy having to give refunds, and we may have to wrestle back the money that was paid as tuition that turned out to be overpriced so we can get outstanding loan balances reduced.

It's common knowledge that the price of a degree has risen faster than inflation. Visual Capitalist has a great chart that shows inflation since 1980 up 236 percent and the price of college over that same time up 1,200 percent.[21] That is solely because of access to debt. Don't believe us? Ask yourself: how many $200,000 worthless degrees would there be if each student had been forced to pay for their tuition in cash before they took the classes? We believe the answer is . . . a lot fewer. We believe loans that were easy to obtain were given out too liberally and that schools took advantage of the situation.

What many people do not realize is that schools with large endowments and other funds, which can amount to billions of dollars, raised tuition rates as quickly as the student loan system could send them more money. In other words, as soon as the government started giving more money to students via loans, the schools hiked their tuition rates.

Therefore, American Laborism will solve the student loan problem by offering anyone who wants a free, unlimited education, opportunity to work to cover their safety-net benefits, and lots of free time to pursue any job they want.

If we need to get specific, consider participating in American Laborism as an opportunity for people deeply in debt to spend one day a week in class, another day a week working for their benefits, and then have five days a week to go into the workforce and earn a paycheck that they can then use to pay off their own loans.

Beyond that, the Advancement Department will partner with any school to offer job placement services to their students if they want to maintain accreditation. It's not fair to students to pay for a degree and then not find work in that field, and the schools that sell overpriced degrees need to take ownership of the problem they pass along to their students.

If it sounds harsh to say that someone with a lot of loans should start working to pay them off, we can assure you that it is not meant to be harsh or any kind of punishment. Because we also believe that the young adults who took out the huge loans did so with the intention of repaying what they borrowed. Sure, there may be some people who borrowed money and never intended to pay it back. We hope those individuals change their mindset. But for those who racked up huge debts, expecting to pay them off after school—this is their chance. Simply sign up for benefits, start attending school, and contribute one day a week, and then work as much as you need in the private sector to reduce your loan balances on your own.

We can help these people by reducing the interest on their loans to 0 percent while they are receiving benefits and making payments. That will help the balance drop faster, and every penny the student pays will go toward principal.

Plus, anyone who is stuck with big loans but can't find work, American Laborism will give them the opportunity to receive education, training, or certification in a field that may prove easier to find fulfilling work in. If part of the problem is that people have expensive degrees with no jobs available, retooling your skills can fix that.

Do all of this, and the problem of student loans of the past will be solved by the borrowers themselves thanks to a combination of paying off the loans they agreed to, participating in existing programs, and allowing students to seek refunds or debt reductions from the schools guilty of overcharging tuition fees.

In twenty years, there will be no student loan problem thanks to American Laborism, because anyone who might have to borrow money to attend school (which the federal government will not participate in) will have the option of free, unlimited education offered to them as an alternative.

We also have no intention of altering the popular G.I. Bill of the US military for providing educational benefits to folks who have served. It's a good program, providing a valuable benefit.

But What About . . .?

Now, let's address what could be, at best, an edge case. What about highly educated people who are uncomfortable thinking other people can get there for free?

We made this one up. It's a negotiating tactic I learned in some strategy book I had to read decades ago. Simply put, you throw out an objection to something that sounds plausible but can easily be knocked down.

The thing is, once we started thinking about this, a lot of complexities and details became apparent, and now we're not sure this can be easily refuted.

We'd all like to think that highly educated people would welcome more educated people joining their ranks. Certainly, it would raise the level of discourse, likely advance current thinking, and add to our collective body of knowledge. It might even challenge accepted doctrines and provide an opportunity for great minds to contribute more than ever before.

Ideally, our society will (in time, of course) enjoy an influx of diverse, highly educated people who take full advantage of unlimited, lifetime education. The same people will then recognize and appreciate the benefits they bring to their own society.

But it's also possible that people who have worked for years, paid huge amounts for education, and felt the effect in their personal, private, or professional lives just might resent others who—thanks to American Laborism—may be seen as having an easier road to achieving the same level of education.

So we won't discount any of that.

But simultaneously, even though this may be a simplified way of looking at it, shouldn't we be willing to pay this price?

And not that we'd want to ever pit newly, highly educated people against their more seasoned, highly educated peers, but it's also a fact that if you find yourself in the latter group, you got there first, and perhaps you can take advantage of that. You have a head start! You have experience! Put it to work!

In summary, the idea that some folks may have paid a lot for their education (maybe, as we just discussed, even went deeply into debt for education) and may not be happy with the idea that American Laborism offers unlimited, free access to education shouldn't hold us back from attempting to advance our society.

Because there are more benefits to American Laborism than just free education (eliminate involuntary poverty and homelessness, reduce taxes, increase the wages millions of people earn, strengthen the military, for example), the perception of unfairness for giving free education that others paid for will have to be something we accept.

People Earn More Thanks to Education

Throughout this chapter, as well as the entire book, we've assumed that education is valuable. In fact, if you felt "receiving education" is the magic bullet that makes the rest of American Laborism succeed, we'd agree. But is that a fair assumption? Does education truly have that much value?

First, let's look at the general concept. We've sprinkled examples throughout the previous chapters, but let's go further. If an individual lacks even basic schooling, such that they can't speak English, which most jobs in America rely upon someone being able to speak and understand, it's easy to see how that individual would benefit from being taught English. No matter what other skills they had, being taught English would make more opportunities available.

Similarly, we can imagine that achieving even a high school-diploma-level of education can increase how much a person's labor is worth. It's actually been measured—how much it pays to increase your level of education. Here's the data that agrees with us: workers' earnings increase as educational attainment rises, according to the US Bureau of Labor Statistics (BLS).[22]

LEVEL OF EDUCATION	MEDIAN USUAL WEEKLY EARNINGS
Doctoral degree	$2,083
Professional degree	$2,080
Master's degree	$1,661
Bachelor's degree	$1,432
Associate's degree	$1,005
Some college, no degree	$935
High school diploma	$853
Less than high school diploma	$682

Figure 2. US Bureau of Labor Statistics, May 2022

What's not listed on the BLS chart is the value of blue-collar jobs. Many of them include trade school and certifications or apprenticeships. Once that's achieved, many of these jobs pay as much or more than degreed jobs. And many blue-collar workers find themselves earning much more quickly as well, rather than waiting years to receive a degree. That's why these kinds of programs, which clearly increase the value of someone's labor, will also be part of American Laborism.

CHAPTER 10

AMERICAN LABORISM AND THE US MILITARY, DEFENSE CONTRACTORS, AND OTHER COMPANIES

Phil

Under American Laborism, you're not paid for the day of work you do to get benefits. But let's say you joined the military. You're not going to get compensated?

Eric

No, that's wrong. The military isn't a safety net. You would be compensated whatever the military sees you're worth, just like it is now.

Phil

So joining the military is not the same as pursuing education to get benefits or asking for benefits and being obliged to pursue education, where the benefits aren't cash. Big difference.

Eric

Correct. For people who don't need benefits, the military hasn't changed at all. For people who need benefits, joining the military may be an option. But the military isn't changing; it's just now one of a shrunken list of options.

The United States Military Plays a Big Role in American Laborism.

Let's get a few important points into the discussion here, so we can have a deeper dive of some specifics throughout the chapter.

First, although we often use the words *the military* throughout this book, it is important to remember that the United States military consists of many branches, and each branch has its own unique culture and traditions.

Second, even if we see an increase in people wanting to join the military, we will not ask the military branches to reduce or compromise their admission standards in any way.

Indeed, we want to be clear that we do not expect the military to lower any of their standards just because they may be called upon to help citizens. We want all of the United States armed services to maintain the highest level of readiness, training, lethality, and ability to carry out their missions as effectively as possible at all times.

Third, we understand that *the military* is currently part of the Department of Defense. We intentionally do not use the name *Department of Defense* as part of what we are keeping. This is not an oversight. Rather, it is because the Department of Defense cannot pass a financial audit, and that means something has to change. This is not political, and you don't have to take our word for it. Senator Ron Wyden (D-OR), chair of the Senate Finance Committee and a supporter of Audit the Pentagon Act, said in 2023, "If the Department of Defense cannot conduct a clean audit, as required by law, Congress should impose tough financial consequences to hold the Pentagon accountable for mismanaging taxpayer money."[23]

It should be noted that this can be immediately solved with blockchain, decentralized ledger technology. If the funds the Department of Defense received were distributed on blockchain, passing an audit would be a breeze.

Hopefully, by the time you read this book, this problem will be behind us. But until that time, we propose that military budgets and expenditures are temporarily handled by a board of citizen advisors from the fields of political and military sciences and accounting with Senate oversight, possibly under the eyes of senators who understand the laws concerning military budgets and support accountability for spending. Each branch of the military has sufficient leadership to function under these conditions.

For whatever reason(s), the Department of Defense can't pass an audit of the trillions of dollars Americans have entrusted it with. We hope having citizen and legislative oversight gets the needed help to straighten out its finances, because the American military is important to America and will perhaps be even more important to American Laborism.

We predict that more people will apply for assistance from the educational part of the American Laborism safety net than from the military or post office. However, we have to be mindful that some people will choose to enlist in the military, so we need to be prepared for that eventuality.

We also want to make sure it's clear that we are aware of the limitations that the Posse Comitatus Act holds to the military branches, which restricts their ability to engage in domestic law enforcement. We are not suggesting there should be any changes to the understanding, enforcement, or adherence of the laws that currently limit the US military's ability to act as a law-enforcement agency within the United States.

We bring that up because, as you'll see (and probably already wondered about), we intend for the US military to provide its unique problem-solving ability to certain American Laborism challenges. It will be within the United States but it won't be law enforcement.

Rather, when you're wondering where we will house people who aren't currently housed, picture the military setting up housing for our citizens in need, which is similar to what they do for themselves all over the world. And of course, that's not all the military can do; they may be able to help Americans with other needs, such as building or improving schools.

American Laborism is providing the building blocks to create real, tangible value for not only individuals who need it most but society as a whole. There are incentives and benefits on a much larger scale to all sectors, including the military, small businesses, and corporations.

In today's rapidly evolving, global landscape, where knowledge and innovation are the driving forces of progress, the importance of educated workers cannot be overstated. Education has the power to shape individuals, transform communities, and revolutionize industries. As we explore the potential benefits of increased education in the military, we uncover a compelling narrative of growth, resilience, and success.

The military, corporations, and small businesses represent distinct sectors, each with its unique demands and challenges. However, they all share a common need for skilled, adaptable, and forward-thinking individuals to navigate the complexities of a rapidly changing world. It is within this context that education becomes paramount, as it is a catalyst for transformation and progress.

In the military, an educated workforce has immense potential for bolstering national security and defense capabilities. Modern warfare requires not only physical prowess but also intellectual agility and strategic thinking. Through education, candidates for the military can gain a deeper understanding of geopolitical dynamics, emerging technologies, and cultural nuances. This knowledge helps them make informed decisions, come up with innovative strategies, and deal effectively with threats. Plus, education creates a sense of discipline, critical thinking, and ethical values, which makes the military better at upholding justice and preserving peace.

Corporations, as engines of economic growth and innovation, benefit significantly from an educated workforce. With so much competition and so many industries being disrupted, companies that succeed will be the ones that embrace education. Well-educated employees bring fresh perspectives, innovative ideas, and the ability to adapt to evolving market demands to their workplace. They are an invaluable asset to any company. Their expertise and problem-solving skills help increase productivity, improve product quality, and make customers happier. Also, education can help develop leadership skills, and companies need to have a pool of leaders who can guide them through changing landscapes.

Small businesses, which are important for economies, also benefit a lot from a more educated workforce. Education gives entrepreneurs and small-business owners the knowledge and skills they need to start, manage, and grow a business successfully. It helps you think like an entrepreneur, understand finances, know marketing, and make decisions effectively. A workforce that's educated within small businesses usually leads to increased competitiveness, operational efficiency, and innovation. In addition, education provides individuals with the skills to become lifelong learners, so they can change with market trends, use technology effectively, and take advantage of new opportunities.

Clearly, increasing education, something that benefits small businesses and corporations, also benefits the military. Education is a catalyst for progress, resilience, and positive transformation. By prioritizing education, we empower individuals to reach their full potential, bridge societal gaps, and contribute meaningfully to their chosen fields, especially if it is to be part of the military.

What about People Who Want to Stay in the Military?

As long as someone meets the military standards, they have the option of staying in military long-term, just as they always have, within the guidelines that work for the military.

We understand that some people who seek federal benefits may believe joining the military will suit them better than going to school. But there isn't guaranteed acceptance into the military, and there is also no guarantee that you can stay in permanently.

We don't think this needs to change from the current system.

However, since literally all federal assistance safety-net aid of any kind will be tied to being in school, it's reasonable to assume that we'll see an influx of people wanting to join the military or working for the post office if going to school is not what they want. In no way should the military (or post office) be seen as a safety net. But they could both be seen as alternatives to the safety net.

This should be an overall positive for the US armed services.

Don't assume the military is obligated to accept every applicant, though. Rather, we will see our military improve over time, because we can be selective with whom we allow to participate.

On top of that, our society—by participating in American Laborism—will gradually become better educated and better trained with more certifications and knowledge. As much as our military draws their recruits from improving citizenry, American Laborism will also have a positive long-term impact on the quality of our military.

Another positive to consider is that even with the trimmed-down federal government, the military budget will be a significant part of annual spending. It may be possible for the size of our military to grow as measured by personnel.

And that will potentially yield benefits to help states and foreign countries that need help. There are already countries around the world who welcome an alliance with America and host military bases that benefit both countries, and these bases can become ambassadors of American Laborism. In fact, if there is any truth to the claims that America is receiving millions of economic and climate migrants from places unsafe to live in, it makes sense to ask our bolstered military to help those countries whose citizens are fleeing.

Having a robust and selective military full of long-term soldiers has many benefits that aren't all related to national defense and security. Of course, it would improve our national defense capacity but also allow the military to expedite humanitarian assistance and disaster response. Disaster support, rescue operations, and medical assistance could be administered on a nationwide scale and not only save lives but minimize severe impacts of these emergencies.

How Does Smaller Government
Affect Defense Contractors?

Earlier, we discussed the efforts of American lawmakers to get clarity and insight into where trillions of US taxpayers' money went after it was budgeted to the Department of Defense. While our laws require every department in the government to pass an audit, the Department of Defense has failed to pass five in a row.[24]

These failed audits have revealed trillions of dollars have been taken from taxpayers and vanished without a trace. This means we cannot accurately track what part of the missing funds were paid to outsiders working with the military, which we will call "defense contractors" for convenience.

Defense contractors can be individuals or organizations, and their role is to provide products or services ranging from military vehicles, water-, air-, and spacecraft, armor and weapons, satellites, computers and electronics, research and development, training, security, logistics and supply-chain support, and communications.

The failed audits mean Americans have no visibility into how our money is spent, but we can also not just eliminate the expenditures, because many of them are critical to the effectiveness of our military and our country's safety.

So we don't have a choice; we need defense contractors.

But we also need the Department of Defense to pass an audit.

The only answer is that the money entrusted to the Department of Defense by US taxpayers must be trackable. By using a blockchain-based version of the dollar, auditors can track the funds and reassure taxpayers and lawmakers that our money is being used properly.

Any defense contractors who want to do business with the United States will have to agree to accept the digital blockchain dollar. This will also allow further tracking of subcontractors and suppliers while preserving the privacy of individuals when it comes to payroll.

You may be shocked to know that there is a technology to track money transfers to the millionth of a penny. (The Department of Defense does not fail its audits because it cannot track the pennies; it fails because it does not track the billions of dollars.)

For this reason, it makes sense to convert every dollar of federal spending into a public ledger living on a blockchain. By utilizing blockchain technology, transactions and data would be decentralized on a clean, traceable ledger. This would not only increase accountability for government spending but also offer various additional advantages. Benefits such as: secure data storage, auditing and compliance, streamlined supply chain management, personal records, and increasing operational efficiency.

Anyone who thinks how the federal government spends our money should not be made public will hate this. They will scream. They will go to war to keep the books private. They will likely even tell you it's their patriotic duty to keep how they spend your money secret, because—I'm predicting—the "terrorists" will know how to defeat us if they can see where we are spending our money.

We don't believe it.

It's yet another place where America is not working in the best interests of Americans.

Before we move on, we are aware of the argument that some Department of Defense, military, and even defense contractor expenditures are intentionally obscured or kept untraceable to protect the identities of people or organizations working with the United States. In many situations, we do in fact need to ensure our partners' anonymity, such as when working with spies or informants. While that may happen and may be legitimate use of funds—and while the audits can certainly accommodate that—we're talking about trillions of missing dollars. It seems unlikely that we're paying spies and informants trillions of dollars.

Solving this is critical, because considering there will only be three departments of the executive branch splitting its portion of the entire federal budget, it's possible that defense contractors could earn a lot of money, assuming the military will have a bigger portion of the pie when other departments get cut.

But remember, the tax rate is dropping to 10 percent. So the amount of money sloshing around might actually decrease.

One thing is certain: by incentivizing the entire country with a lower tax rate of 2 percent as soon as the federal debt is paid off, you should expect much tighter financial controls. (Say goodbye to the $600 hammers!)

Therefore, Laborism, if it is to work, will be transparent. Remember, we aren't giving the citizens most in need in our country untraceable, unauditable cash benefits, even though it would admittedly be easier and much more convenient.

So why would the defense contractors be held to a different standard?

There is no legitimate reason we can think of for Americans to not be able to trace *every* dollar of tax money and how it is spent. To provide the most benefits to the most people, we will be tracing all the taxes that come in and the expenditures that go out.

Don't worry about the privacy issue, though. Blockchain can do this without revealing or risking the exposure of anyone's private and personally identifying information.

To any defense contractors or other businesses that wish to be paid by the federal government, we welcome you. Just know that the population is now highly encouraged to reduce waste and track every penny they pay you.

But What About . . .?

You may be asking, "But what about businesses, corporations, and public companies? How will American Laborism impact them?"

Defense contractors would not be the only companies to reap

the rewards of American Laborism. That's right—it's not all about AI and defense companies. All sectors of the corporate world can not only participate but also benefit significantly.

Corporations may have a beneficiary role in the acceptance of American Laborism.

It should go without saying that once Laborism begins to take effect and people have access to as much education as they want, all companies of any size that hire people will benefit from a continuously improving workforce.

People will receive education and training as part of their benefits, and companies will have more, better-qualified potential employees.

Companies who currently offer employees tuition reimbursement or other benefits designed to encourage personal development will have the option of coordinating this with schools. It could be a win-win scenario where the employee keeps their job, with one day a week counted toward receiving educational benefits with a participating school, a day of classes, and the company paying the employee a higher wage due to not having to pay for the educational benefit. Sure, this may be in the future, but it's a possible benefit for everyone involved.

With a competitive, highly educated workforce, there are many advantages that only drive society forward. We are looking at a serious improvement in productivity that will allow people to perform tasks much more efficiently. Well-trained workers have a stronger understanding of their roles, become effective industry leaders, require less guidance or supervision, and can quickly adapt to technological changes while boosting productivity within the company.

Let's conclude this section with entrepreneurship and innovation. Educated individuals have increased critical thinking skills and can generate new, innovative ideas while developing unique solutions to modern challenges. People who start their own businesses should also benefit from this. Not the least of these reasons is that people who have their most basic needs met (by American Laborism) may choose to take the exciting step toward independence and risk starting their own business.

Imagine the effect on our society when millions of people pull themselves up into the entrepreneur and business-owner category.

We also anticipate that corporations will either create new internship programs or expand the ones they already use, in coordination with the schools, to place people who contribute labor into positions where they fit the best.

And we have a great plan to incentivize corporations all the way, from smaller, locally owned shops to large national businesses, to participate and provide labor services on a massive scale.

That's because American Laborism will radically rewrite the corporate tax code, eliminating virtually all deductions for anything other than labor costs.

This change may have to be implemented gradually, as companies have been making capital and equipment investments based on current tax codes. We anticipate shifting from the current corporate tax system to the new one over the course of ten years, for example.

In time, there's no doubt that businesses and companies who hire people will start maximizing their processes based not on complicated tax benefits but rather on maximizing their use of labor. Only the companies who are abusing the current tax system with loopholes will have a problem with this. And frankly, that's a price we're willing to pay to achieve what Laborism is setting out to achieve.

American Laborism will show its true symbiosis with companies while simultaneously employing people, the main goal of Laborism.

CHAPTER 11

ECONOMICS VS. POLITICS

IF YOU WERE to ask most Americans how they feel about our entrenched two-party system, you might be surprised how divided it has forced us to become.

What happened to that lofty ideal that both political parties drag out and repeat *ad nauseam* during their campaigns? You know the one: the claim that we need to "come together as one" (almost always immediately followed by a smear of the other side).

If these political parties had our best interests in mind, this system is a no-brainer. As we've said before, we believe American Laborism is a *purple* system. By that, we mean there are aspects of our economic system that will appeal to both red- and blue-identifying citizens. Both liberals and conservatives. Both folks who want to provide more services for the needy as well as folks who want to eliminate our deficit, pay off our debts, and reduce our taxes.

But just implementing American Laborism at the federal level—as purple as it is—may leave some citizens still unable to come together and be happy with the solution we've provided.

As you'll see from the following, that doesn't invalidate American Laborism. Thanks to America's design from our founding (that of individual states having their own determination in many areas), we don't all have to agree with everything for it to still work.

Plus, as we've already seen, states can opt to increase or decrease services and taxes anyway.

Will Some States Want to Further Restrict Their Citizens?

Why would we ask this? Is this even a real possibility?

Actually, it might be. Because if American Laborism has the

intended effect of dramatically reducing the federal government, and as a result, some programs that people want are cut, then it's possible that the states might pick them up.

And that, at first, might sound like a good thing. It may be. But we need to remember the discussion we had about people who constantly ask the government for financial benefits, programs, or services. We used the notion of possibly walking to your neighbor's house and asking for something versus asking the government, which has taken on an almost omnipresent yet undefinable role, of being *something* but not being *us*. In other words, the government has become something that is all-present but also undefined and removed from the people.

Every time anyone utters the phrase "The government should pay for . . . ," they acknowledge that there is a cost associated with the implementation of whatever the next part is.

If we move any program to a state level, then the impact of that program, both positive and negative, will be felt by people on a much more local scale. And the cost is also moved one step closer to the people.

Here's what we mean. Let's assume American Laborism has rolled out and is operating as expected nationwide. Anyone who needs safety-net help from the federal government, such as an unemployed worker or someone previously receiving food stamps or welfare, have signed up for benefits. They've been enrolled in at least a day of education, and they've begun providing a day of labor to their school, community, or wherever they are the best fit. Plus, they're receiving food, shelter, suitable clothing, all their school materials, and anything they need for their job.

And obviously, since their minimum contribution only requires two days per seven-day week, they have plenty of time to do any extra studying, working for pay, or even relaxing.

But let's imagine two neighboring states see what has happened differently. Let's imagine the leaders of one state—we'll say New Mexico—want all their citizens to have a mobile phone and access to the Internet as part of the state's minimum basic services. And for the sake of discussion, let's imagine that the neighboring state Arizona decides the federal minimum American Laborism safety net is sufficient.

Let's not assume Arizona is mean, uncaring, cheap, or anti-technology. Perhaps the political leaders of Arizona see that folks who aren't on the safety net but want a mobile phone and Internet service have all paid for their own, and Arizona decides, in fairness, they won't be providing these extra phones and service. With people having five days per week free and clear of obligation, Arizona might believe that those who want a phone can take on extra work—for pay, of course—and get their own phone—just like the non-safety-net folks, as we mentioned. This could actually be seen as Arizona treating its citizens fairly.

But back in New Mexico, perhaps the leaders think it's fairer to provide phones and services to even the people who aren't paying for them. So the New Mexico government votes for and passes appropriations for this extra device and service. It then contracts with a provider to ensure that everyone in the safety net gets a device and Internet service at no cost.

No cost to the recipient, that is.

We're all smart enough to know that devices and services have a cost. And since New Mexico provides it, New Mexican taxpayers will eventually foot the bill. When this all plays out, the cost of providing free phones will be borne by New Mexico state taxpayers, not the actual users.

And if New Mexicans are OK with that . . . so is American Laborism. You could argue that having a citizenry who can all stay in touch—even though the cost has shifted away from the citizen and to the state—is worth it.

So, notice this interesting paradox that develops. The more a state or municipality may want to give to its citizens, the more they'll have to restrict those citizens by taking their money through taxation. And here's why: saying the state *gives* you anything is flat-out wrong.

We *are* the state. Or at least we should be! Therefore, if we want to further restrict ourselves beyond the small number of services offered by the federal government, we can. If a state wants to recreate all the programs we closed, they can. And their voters can approve it.

We may have started with a simple example of a mobile device and Internet service, but it isn't hard to see how—after two-and-a-half centuries of voting ourselves on ever-increasing government programs—we've arrived at where America is now, where our leaders are creating programs, laws, and taxes that aren't always in our best interest.

Before we close this section, we'll ask you a question: how many programs, wars, expenditures, departments, agencies, and boondoggles that have thrust us well over $30 trillion in debt can you list right now as something you absolutely could not have lived without? We'll wager that most honest citizens can't account for more than a trillion dollars of expenditures they deem worth going into permanent debt over. That's how big we've allowed our government to get.

But if states see this differently, if they prefer the wasteful expenditures our government has been making (or simply feel people shouldn't have to work for mobile devices and Internet connection), then they can localize the expenses of these programs.

But American Laborism is striving to reduce the size and cost (and waste!) of government while increasing the value of the services it provides, so increasing taxes and questionable programs will be handled by the states by voting to tax their residents more if they wish. And we'd bet a trillion dollars that those increased taxes will likely be quite progressive.

In summary, those states that opt to increase taxes are, in fact, restricting the citizens who pay those taxes!

Will There Be a Living Wage or UBI?

Around this time in the discussion, you might be thinking, *Will there be any kind of "living wage" or "universal basic income"?*

Any form of *universal basic income* (or UBI, a guaranteed cash benefit paid to every citizen from the federal government without any need to work or means test) will not be part of American Laborism under any circumstance as a federal benefit.

However, if you reframe the concept from *universal basic income* to *universal* basic benefits* . . . now you're talking. (I'll explain the asterisk soon.)

What's the difference?

First, there won't be any federal cash benefits under Laborism. Zero. None. Not even the questionable little "experiments" that some governments and politicians are floating out as tests, just so they can get people thinking it's possible for a country to pay its citizens for simply existing.

Second, paying people to do nothing is the opposite of American Laborism.

Well, except for the Alaska Permanent Fund Dividend. That's the closest we can find to a system that pays Americans (who live in Alaska) . . . just because. The truth of that dividend is that it comes from the Alaska Permanent Fund, which is funded by the extraction of oil from under Alaska, which is then transported through the Trans-Alaska Pipeline System.

This example of Alaska's permanent fund payments shows clearly what has to happen for UBI to work: there has to be a literal surplus of resources. In this case, the funding comes from the process of extracting oil from the ground, transporting it, and using it for oil and petroleum-based products, including oil and gas fossil fuels.

That means the only UBI program actually functioning in America is contributing to our use of fossil fuels. How do you feel about that? Excited? Neutral? Disgusted? We're willing to bet that most people who want a universal basic income in America hadn't realized this fact. We won't go any further with this because the point is made—extracting and using oil is the only successful "pay to exist" program ever launched in America.

If you're a big fan of UBI and believe there is more to it than literally paying people an income without requiring them to contribute, please tell us how.

With that out of the way, here's why we think *universal* *basic benefits* (UBB) are better than *universal basic income*. And this is where that little asterisk comes into play. We append *universal* because while American Laborism can provide universal benefits, we don't believe everyone will need or want them. That's a good thing! So they're *universal* in that American Laborism will cover all of someone's basic human needs plus unlimited, free education for life—*if* you want them and *if* you participate in school and *if* you contribute a fair amount of labor—so there is no need for UBI. Most people, though, probably want more than the *basic* human needs. Who wants to maintain a *minimal* lifestyle forever? So you can take all the free education and then go get an excellent, good-paying job that matches your giftedness and interests.

If you want *income* (or capital), then American Laborism encourages you to go out and get some.

It just won't be from us.

But Socialists and Communists Aren't Willing to Let Go of Control

We believe that people who identify as Marxists, socialists, and communists, and who are honest about what appeals to them about collectivist ideas, will find something to love about American Laborism. With that said, some people might see our policies and think that we have adopted communist, socialist, or Marxist principles, but that is absolutely not the case.

The truth is, Americans who have the benefit of living in our capitalist society (as imperfect as it is) yet yearn for an imagined collectivist society that has never existed are deluding themselves. Their acceptance of American Laborism will only happen if they are willing to adopt the mindset that everyone who wants benefits will have to pitch in some labor and attend school.

More importantly, anyone who doesn't want to live in a collectivist manner can simply choose to pay their taxes and not contribute more than that.

This is an opt-in system, with no forced participation. That right there is the biggest, most indelible, impossible-to-ignore differentiator between American Laborism and any kind of Marxism system—nobody is forced to work, and nobody gets benefits "for free." (Plus, American Laborism respects the right to private property!)

When we said earlier that labor is better than capital, we were being completely serious. If you talk to someone who actually lives in a true socialist/communist country, you should ask them how satisfied they are with their quality of life. While you're at it, inquire if there is a relatively small group of individuals with tremendous wealth and control in that country with disproportionate power. Just for an added bonus, try to find significant innovation and economic success stories from said country while it was under this control.

That said, those unwilling to participate in Laborism will not be able to rely on the federal government for handouts or assistance.

It's important to remember that state and local governments are perfectly within their rights to enact soul-crushing, productivity-killing communism if that's what the voters want. They can increase taxes and force their residents to comply with collectivist practices, which typically encourage people to do as little as possible to get by. If a state—perhaps California—wanted to pay a universal basic income to all citizens, tax only the wealthiest, and provide generous benefits to residents without any kind of work require-ments, it would be possible to do so. That is California's option.

We obviously don't think it's a great idea, but we'd be surprised if some state doesn't attempt to adopt increasingly Marxist policies in a misguided belief that what people need is more government and less personal accountability.

And yes, frankly, we expect politicians—even Democratic Socialists—will have a hard time minimizing their own desire for control over people. Think about it: communism, the economic system that purports to offer equality and take care of everyone, is virtually forced to be managed in an authoritarian way. That's because soon after Marxist economics are forced upon people, anyone who doesn't like it has no choice but to participate or, often, be punished or even killed if they don't agree with the system.

In order for collectivists to create the change they want to see, they will have to be willing to let go of what they believe is their power. Although it may be difficult, it is worth it because American Laborism has the potential to be great. If a person believes in the "take care of each other" theories behind collectivism, American Laborism offers that.

But it also lets people live an honest life, in that if someone doesn't want to be part of a collective, they don't have to.

Some People Aren't Wealthy but Simply Want to Punish Wealthy People by Way of Taxation

We're anticipating that progressive taxes—which are taxes where the rate of taxation increases as income increases—will be hard for some people to give up under the American Laborism system.

For some, it may be impossible. Progressive taxes are discrim-inatory in that they treat two individuals differently, but the notion that this type of discrimination is acceptable, fair, and even noble has sadly become deeply ingrained in the American psyche.

We'd even argue that a significant number of Americans aren't even capable of imagining living under a taxation plan that doesn't "punish those who earn more." It's sad, really.

Decades—perhaps even a century—of progressive leaders exclaiming "it's only fair" if the rich pay more . . . the rich can afford it . . . the wealthy deserve to support the poor . . . have had the effect of skewing what the definition of "fair" is.

Think about it this way: if you were to ask any American if they believed in fairness, the answer would almost universally be yes. For decades, psychologists have been investigating fairness from different angles—not just looking at whether the outcome is fair, but also studying people's perceptions of fairness and even delving into the fairness of the procedures used to arrive at an outcome. Americans obsess over fair play in our sports. We fully expect that the companies we deal with will treat us in a completely fair manner. We even have customs and expectations for how to quit a job in a fair and reasonable way!

But convincing Americans that a flat tax rate is unfair and progressive taxes are fair is another way America has failed Americans.

It is impossible for everyone to be equal in the eyes of the federal government if the law requires some people to pay a higher percentage of their income and assets as taxes than other people. America, for more than a century, has been exacerbating the division between our people every year on April 15 like clockwork. (This is the date when Americans are required to file their taxes.)

More correctly, that's when—under capitalism—*half* of Americans pay their taxes. The other half? Nope. For years, America has perpetuated the false belief that some of its citizens are unable to take care of themselves or their basic needs and, as a result, have to depend on the wealth of those classified as "rich."

This is poison.

And we don't mean it's poison just to the rich. Far worse, it's poisonous to the people who believe they shouldn't participate in paying for government services. Over time, it can be heartbreaking to constantly be told by your government that you're not good enough or don't have what it takes to contribute.

And people who believe in progressive taxes keep it going.

But at least for the federal taxation, this is ending now.

People who want to crank up taxes on the wealthy and high earners will have to do it at the state level. Under Laborism, the federal government will absolutely not have a progressive tax scheme.

However, at the state level, should a group of people want to enact taxes that take a larger portion of income from a subset of their residents, they are welcome to do it.

But we want no part of it.

An Immediate End to Tax Loopholes

In 2017, the political fact-checking website Politifact ran an article titled "[the United States Federal] Tax code is so long that nobody's really sure of its length."[25] The context behind the article was politicians debating whether our tax code, the laws that govern how much of our earned income we give to the IRS every year, had grown too big—which we take to mean it is working against the interest of Americans.

Politifact noted the tax code itself is 6,550 pages long but that there are as many as 66,000 pages of case law *related* to the tax code. That was in 2017. Numerous changes have been added since then (and some of those don't even start until 2025).

Now, it makes sense that *if* those thousands of pages held a flawless tax plan that perfectly served every American, the length wouldn't matter. But they come nowhere near that. Rather, these innumerable pages hold a maze of rules so complex that most of us believe the current code contains loopholes that allow some of our neighbors and some American companies to avoid paying their fair share of taxes.

Under American Laborism, states and municipalities can enact whatever taxes they want, but we believe the only tax write-off at the federal level should be the cost of labor.

There would be no loopholes because there would be no deductions, other than anyone who pays for labor being able to deduct the cost of that labor. Companies wanting to maximize deductions would have the option of paying more for labor. Clearly, with a 10 percent tax rate, you don't pay $100 in labor to save $10 in taxes. You would pay $100 in labor to get productivity and profits . . . but not merely for the potential of a tax break. But let's say, if the corporation decided it wanted to game the system and not pay as much in taxes, it'd have to drastically increase how much it's paying for labor, which in turn works to its employees' benefit. And the people who receive that payment for labor obviously owe income tax.

So the loopholes we'd look for would be a company pretending to pay for labor while it spends its money on something else, an organization generating kickbacks from overpaying for labor, and so on. With only one deductible—labor—that's the only scheme or loophole you'd need to watch for.

But that means the newly reduced tax code won't allow any deduction for the write-off or expensing of labor-saving devices at all. If a company feels it wants to invest in labor-saving devices or labor-saving technologies, it can, of course, but it won't be able to deduct or depreciate the cost to try to reduce the taxes it pays.

There's a simple reason for that, and it's that an economy attempting to raise the value of labor shouldn't subsidize reducing how much labor is needed.

For example, say a salesperson visits a factory, trying to sell the business owner on the benefits of a new piece of technology. The salesperson proudly exclaims, "This machine can do the work of forty people!"

To which the factory owner replies, "Why would I want to put forty people out of a job?"

If we respect labor and the people who provide their labor, and if we believe it's respectable and worth participating in this, then it makes sense to remove any incentive that anybody has for a labor-saving device.

But you might think we've overlooked the possibility that this would limit technology and innovation. You might wonder if it is reasonable to intentionally stifle innovation that necessarily increases productivity, efficiency, worker safety, and profits. Further, if America had always operated under this mindset, would we have achieved all that we have so far?

We haven't overlooked those at all. In fact, chapter 14 specifically calls for American innovation to help us accomplish American Laborism because if we focus on labor, we will get different innovations than if we focus on capital accumulation.

Rather than stifling innovation, we believe we would be purifying and refocusing it. Purifying in the sense that innovation for increased productivity, efficiency, worker safety, and profits will be refocusing away from mere capital accumulation and toward better labor conditions.

Increasing productivity is a good incentive, but not if it triggers a race to the bottom for the value of labor. Labor-saving can still be deployed to increase your bottom line, increase your shareholder value, and increase your free cash flow, but your tax bill won't be reduced by a federal government whose job is to maintain dignified production of labor from everyone.

American Laborism creates a world where companies compete for workers, rather than people competing for work. We'll remind you that a benefit of an economy focused on labor is that a person's *labor* is different from a person's *capital.* If you're concerned that it sounds un-American for the federal government to possibly "reward" businesses for limiting innovation and efficiency because they employ a lot of people rather than robots, for example, we have a solution for your concern. If it sounds like we're saying the federal government favors companies with bloated payrolls, limited innovation (and therefore limited production), higher overhead (due to paid labor), and lower profits (again, due to high overhead), this should appease your worries: labor isn't unlimited.

When payrolls are full, everyone who wants a job has a job, and our economy is, well, working, we will see companies streamlining, innovating, improving, and even competing, all for more or better labor.

The tax part of American Laborism will be fair and equal, and it will be expensive to try to cheat the system.

Imagine a friendly dog that wags its tail and fetches balls if you feed it—but bites you if you don't. In this analogy, the government is the dog, and our tax money is the food. And if we don't pay our taxes, the governments bites.

Loopholes and tax cheats are created when the tax code gets too aggressive. This is because people always try to find ways to minimize their tax burden.

Under American Laborism, with extremely low and equal tax rates for all citizens and residents, there will be very little need for loopholes and no incentive to cheat. We won't have a complicated tax code that incentivizes citizens to try to game their way out of paying taxes. And because we're charging a low rate, we'll eliminate mortgage interest deductions (we know it's popular, but we're more than $30 trillion in debt!). Another tax change will be to completely eliminate any deductions any company might want to take for investing in any device or technology that serves the purpose of reducing how much labor the company needs to employ.

If a company wants to reduce its labor expenses in a society that (now) values labor, there's no chance at all that it should qualify for tax breaks. Because a tax break means the rest of society is paying more (since you're paying less) and the result is . . . less labor! In fact, you can look at deductions or depreciation or expensing labor-saving devices as a double societal cost: the cost of reduced tax revenue plus the cost to society of reducing how many people are working.

We're not saying that we will restrict companies from buying or investing in labor-saving devices or technologies—but we certainly won't socialize the cost by reducing their taxes for it.

Remember, we propose that we start with a tax plan that has companies paying the same 10 percent tax as individuals and allows only one deduction from a company's profits: the cost of labor.

Nothing else. No amount of fancy accounting can create loopholes. And in fact, all loopholes that have worked their way into the tax code will just disappear.

But here's the good news: companies won't need loopholes. That's because even at a flat 10 percent corporate income tax and 0.25 percent annual wealth (or assets) tax, their tax burden is going to plunge.

In 2021, the United States Treasury released a report that calculated the taxes of corporations of the thirty-eight countries in the Organization for Economic Co-operation and Development (OECD), an international organization that works to create better government policies and improve peoples' lives.

The study found that in 2021 (the most recent data released[26]), only seven member countries collected a higher Effective Average Tax Rate (EATR) for corporations in their jurisdiction than the US does. America, with our 25.9 percent EATR, has such high corporate taxes that over three-quarters of OECD countries collect less from corporations.

But when American Laborism changes all our taxes—even corporations—to 10 percent, America's corporate income tax burden would drop to literally the lowest of all OECD countries. *Fortune* magazine reports that American companies' pre-tax profits were $2.8 trillion in 2021, so doing some quick math, American Laborism would reduce their income tax burden by $445 billion if they paid 10 percent American Laborism income taxes instead of 25.9 percent, the figure the US Treasury calculated for current income taxes.

Even considering the new yearly 0.25 percent assets tax American Laborism will be levying, it's still a great deal. That's because according to the Federal Reserve Board of Governors, American nonfinancial corporations hold an estimated $58.7 trillion in assets on their balance sheets. Taxing them 0.25 percent on those comes to about $146.75 billion . . . so they'd be *saving* almost $300 billion a year.

That would be an amazing incentive for companies that have been considering leaving America due to our high tax burden to stay. And it would be a powerful magnet to draw companies to America if they wanted to escape high taxes elsewhere. Perhaps it would set off a competition that countries around the world would work to reduce their tax burdens and shrink their own governments. Wouldn't that be great?

And before you start to worry that reducing corporate taxes by $300 billion will cost too much lost revenue to the Treasury, take a minute to refresh yourself on one of the most exciting byproducts of lower taxes: higher tax revenue.

The Laffer Curve is an analysis from 1979 created by economist Art Laffer, in which he describes how higher tax *rates* can reduce tax *revenues* as taxpayers decide to forgo work and earning because the tax burden is stifling. And, as you can imagine, it works in reverse too. Lower tax rates not only pour more money back to the bottom line of the taxpayer but also into the economy and investments, which create growth and more income, which is also taxed.

And Art Laffer didn't even have the rising value of the community's labor from American Laborism to take into consideration.

But now, let's look at companies and individuals who think they can avoid paying taxes by cheating.

Cheating, first and foremost, will be seen as a literal expression of thinking our laws don't apply to you. That's not how healthy countries or communities stay healthy. If everyone is paying their fair share and a cheater is not, how are they not essentially stealing from everyone who is following the rules?

Second, the incentive not to cheat must be convincing; it has to be more trouble than it's worth, a risk not worth taking. But not cheating also has to be something that is seen as acceptable within our society.

So the Laborism federal taxes will be 10 percent on income—all income, dividends, capital gains, interest, value added, literally everything—until our federal debt is paid off. After that, the tax rate plunges to 2 percent on income.

Plus, we'll be collecting one quarter of one percent—that's 0.25 percent—on everything everyone and every company owns on their balance sheet each year. Everything.

Yes, we know there's an argument to be made that if you pay a tax on something, you don't own it. We get that. It's not entirely wrong.

But it's also not wrong to say that a law-abiding society taking care of our needy citizens and residents is worth paying for. Moreover, our country is over $30 trillion in debt. How could someone argue that paying taxes means they don't really own their property, then turn around and ignore the fact that being deeply in debt doesn't mean the exact same thing?

But there is more to this than just emotional arguments about "needy citizens" or logical arguments about "we're all deeply in debt."

Think purely pragmatically for a second, and realize the value of common defense of property rights.

If you think that paying a yearly wealth tax of only 0.25

percent is unfair, we would like to try to convince you otherwise. Many people in America may feel the same way, as this is a new concept, but we believe that given the chance, we could change your perspective. For those of you who read a lot, you are probably aware that wealth taxes have been tried before in Europe and they were not received well by the public. This hasn't escaped us. Now, to be clear, all the proposed wealth taxes we know of had tax rates that were multiple times higher than the rates we are suggesting.

Here's how we can make a wealth tax—which would charge a tiny amount on everything you own—more palatable to the public: by making property rights sacrosanct and by providing common defense.

Here's what this means. American Laborism, much like capitalism, believes in the individual ownership of property. You own what you own, and you can keep what you own—subject to that 0.25 percent annual wealth tax. A key element of the social contract in America is that everyone pays taxes, and in return, the government is responsible for defending the rights of its citizens. So if someone doesn't want to pay taxes, why would they expect the government to defend any of their rights? Would they prefer to build a moat and an impenetrable wall around their property to ensure no one encroaches on their land? Would they prefer to issue their own currency, or would they rather barter with their neighbors? Will they travel by jetpack so they can avoid the interstate system? Naturally, don't expect to have access to American Laborism safety-net services, free education, post office deliveries, or the US military defending your property if you don't want to pay for those services.

We're using silly examples to make the point that, while nobody will want a wealth tax, we believe the value of paying it and paying for the common services our country provides is worth it.

United States Federal Reserve data from 2023 calculated that US citizens and nonprofit organizations owned more than $148.8

trillion in wealth.[27] A quarter of a percent wealth tax will only cost its owners about $372 billion a year. That's equivalent to paying $2.50 when you own $1,000 (and because we believe in fair taxes, people with $1,000 will indeed pay $2.50 in wealth tax).

Want to get out from under that 0.25 percent tax? Pay off the national debt, then we'll talk.

Now, how do we disincentivize people and companies who cheat on their taxes?

Easy. If you're caught not paying American Laborism taxes, you'll be penalized with the tax rate paid by the top marginal earners during the last US presidential administration to run a budget surplus: that of William Jefferson Clinton, the forty-second president of the United States of America.

That's right, there hasn't been a federal budget surplus since 2001. And since it's a goal of American Laborism to pay off our debt, which requires a surplus, it's fitting that anyone who doesn't want to pay American Laborism taxes will pay Clinton taxes . . . with a twist.

The twist is, the top marginal tax rate of 2001 will be applied to everything you earn and own in the year you are caught cheating. To make it simple, the same penalty will apply to cheating individuals and cheating companies.

That rate is 39.1 percent.

If you don't want to pay 10 percent now (or 2 percent when our debt is eventually paid off), then expect to pay 39.1 percent. That 39 percent will be the punishment rate for anyone—and everyone—caught attempting to shirk, loophole, avoid, minimize, or otherwise cheat on their taxes.

And if you're caught cheating a second time? The penalty will be no more than the top marginal tax bracket under another popular Democrat president, Franklin D. Roosevelt. Under his administration, the top marginal tax rate was 94 percent. Therefore, tax cheats who try again after being caught and subjected to 39.1 percent tax on all their earnings and wealth will—as their second offense—be taxed 94 percent of their income and wealth.

Yes, that is a ridiculously high penalty. We shudder to think that someone would even risk it. Hardly seems worth it!

Honestly, though, we'd rather everyone pay exactly what they owe and not a penny more or less. One of the core beliefs of American Laborism is that taxes should be low, flat, and fair. After we pay off our national debt, at which time we switch to a 2 percent tax, we can consider eliminating the wealth tax. But to do this, we need to eliminate loopholes, tax avoidance, and tax cheats. Hopefully, by having extremely high penalties for cheaters, we won't have many cheaters.

The Internal Revenue Service, with so much less to do, will be folded into the post office to collect taxes from citizens and corporations, with advisories and innovation from both the Advancement and Military Departments as a joint effort.

Let us add a side note: If we are to achieve the final stated goal of American Laborism—that being 2 percent income taxes—at our current GDP levels, the taxes collected wouldn't be enough to pay what we spent on the military in 2022. We're aware of this hypothetical shortfall—it hasn't escaped us. So how would we handle that?

First, the government will have to satisfactorily prove that all military expenditures are legitimate. That hasn't been completed satisfactorily in the recent past, but converting to blockchain tracking of our entire federal executive branch will immediately solve this problem.

Should all expenditures prove to be legitimate and necessary, something will have to change to prevent shortfalls. There's only one solution that doesn't require cutting military budgets, which we are against. That is to grow GDP faster than we grow the military budget. If we can hold military spending increases to 2 percent per year and grow our GDP by 4 percent per year, in just thirty years, we'll be able to pull this off! We've talked about paying off the federal debt throughout the book and that doing so will trigger a dramatic decrease in taxes; this quick analysis would indicate that although the task of paying off so much debt may seem impossible, we think having a thirty-year target to do so makes it possible.

As long as increasing everyone's education, lowering their taxes (and closing the loopholes!), and reducing the size and scope of our very expensive government all come together to grow America, we can do this.

CHAPTER 12

FOREVER IMPROVING FOREIGN AFFAIRS

AMERICAN LABORISM is predominantly focused on domestic, American issues and how they can be improved. That means America will take a decidedly different role in world affairs and international relations.

The most simple, basic explanation of what to expect can be easily summarized: the era of guiding foreign policy with cash payments will change. Instead, we will begin to see a shift in how countries relate to one another.

However, we are not suggesting that all America's foreign policy is based on cash payments. Over the past century, America's foreign policy has become increasingly complex, blending all the different tools and resources at America's disposal. To put it simply, we've ranged from cash support, supplies and equipment, economic ties, economic sanctions, political influence, military aid and intervention, and (experts suggest) even covert operations.

Recently, our foreign policy has become so convoluted that there has been discussion among American citizens that it appears as if our country is supporting both sides of a conflict, or people and policies we fundamentally disagree with, or even giving aid to areas that turn around and use it against us.

Some of that—or none of it—may be true. The truth is, most American citizens are only vaguely aware of their own country's foreign involvement.

When it comes to American Laborism, expect all this to change.

It would likely surprise no one that if our federal government is reduced to military, education, and post office, the only tools available to us for foreign involvement will then necessarily be armed services, school, and mail.

If we get rid of cash payments to our own citizens (and only give them in-kind benefits), it would make sense for our foreign policy to be the same: no more cash payments.

We'll talk about foreign affairs more, but only briefly, as that is not the biggest concern of American Laborism. To those readers who believe that the world needs American financial aid in order to survive, we say this: remember that we, as a country, are in debt. Our children and grandchildren will end up paying back every dollar we have sent out of the country. And while some (certainly not all) of America's foreign assistance expenditures may have been for noble and worthy purposes, we're still spending more money than we are producing each year, and that has to stop.

With that in mind, we're not talking about complete isolationism, as you'll see. With our new focus on education, we can boost study-abroad opportunities. And because our economy will be retooled to value labor, our foreign policy can shift to see us providing labor when our allies need help instead of capital.

With the most powerful all-volunteer military we've ever had, we can seek opportunities to partner with countries by placing bases or other military facilities where they are strategically helpful. And if a country needs help, rather than sending them money, we can deploy troops and their expertise to help.

What Happens to Foreign Aid?

It's going to drastically change, as we just mentioned.

Under American Laborism, any and all foreign aid will be provided in the same manner as all domestic federal aid: militarily, educationally, or by supplying labor.

Your first thought might be that supplying labor sounds simplistic because of logistical challenges, or how could someone who is only obligated to work one day a week perform that job in a foreign country?

Wouldn't sending dollars be so much easier, more efficient, and possibly even safer than sending people to help with labor?

Take a longer-term view. You may not believe us when we say this, but the practice of sending US dollars—now viewed as an efficient way to "send help"—had to earn that acceptance over decades. American historians likely recall that the first instance of America providing foreign aid to another country was in 1812. The aid went to Venezuela, which suffered from an earthquake that caused terrible damage to Caracas, the country's capital, while Venezuela was also fighting for its independence from Spain. America authorized $50,000 for the effort, but the aid was sent not as cash, but as food.[28]

Obviously, over two hundred years ago, sending US dollars (USD) wouldn't have had the same effect as sending food, which people could immediately benefit from.

Over the decades, as the US economy grew, we began to trade with a growing number of countries around the world, and gradually many of them began to accept payments in dollars for the goods we were importing from them.

Think about it: virtually any item that you own or use that was made in another country is likely due to the proliferation of the USD. As America grew, so did the acceptance and use of the US dollar.

In time, nongovernmental organizations (NGOs) and charitable aid organizations, such as the Red Cross and Red Crescent (as well as many others), found that when they were rushing to help disaster-stricken areas, sometimes dollars could move faster than food and medical supplies. And there's little argument that having available dollars for solving problems allows you flexibility. If you need medicine, it might be easier to buy medicine with dollars, rather than having to convert generously donated food and clothing into the medicine you need.

The dollar is accepted virtually everywhere.

A large part of that is due to America's choice of deploying our dollars as official foreign policy. During World War I, America helped Belgium with $387 million.[29] Much of that aid was in the form of loans, and most of those were forgiven after the war. Other examples include after World War II, when America provided nearly $2 billion of aid to countries such as China, Czechoslovakia, Greece, Italy, Poland, the Ukrainian SSR, and Yugoslavia (as they were known at the time), which suffered from the war.[30]

Another post-WWII economic aid program saw America help its allies under the Marshall Plan with over $15 billion in aid.[31]

There are countless examples, including current foreign aid, as well as likely countless others that haven't been well-publicized. The point we're trying to make is that the pathway for aid from America taking the form of US dollars was spread over time, and we'd argue that the acceptance of the USD as a form of aid only grew because the American economy was strong relative to most of the world. Our currency was gradually accepted more and more, eventually even becoming sought after and preferred.

But America can't count on this lasting forever. Sadly, another example of America not working in the best interests of Americans is our increasingly poor financial management of our country.

Since 2001, we haven't had a balanced federal budget or budgetary surplus. We're $30 trillion in debt (at least!) and currently operating under a budgetary framework that allows unlimited spending at least until 2025.

America spends more than America makes. It's entirely possible that the strength of the US dollar will soon come into question because so many of them are now in circulation.

That's disappointing because America is generous with our foreign aid. There were twenty-four federal departments or agencies for which we could track foreign aid spending in 2020. Between them, they sent over $51 billion of aid. That includes the US Agency for International Development, the Department of Defense, the State Department, the Department of Health and Human Services, the Department of the Treasury, the Peace Corps, and many more.[32]

It's beyond the scope of this book, but we're not entirely convinced that our politicians, departments, and various agencies always provide thorough accounting of where their budgets are going. It's possible there are programs and expenditures that increase how much we spend overseas, but without more accurate accounting—the kind that decentralized ledger technology or blockchain can provide—we may never know how much is being spent on anything our government does, unfortunately.

For anyone wondering what will happen with those twenty-four departments and agencies, all with their own expenditures for foreign aid (such as the State Department), when we reduce the government to just three departments, the answer is that all their diplomatic functions that pertain to foreign interaction and foreign aid will be assumed by the military. Ideally, integrating the State Department into the military will yield a more diplomatic military, and they'll use that skill often.

There are many advantages to that. The most obvious is that America can hone and maintain a unified voice and strategy in foreign affairs. More pragmatically, it makes sense that all aid should be efficiently managed.

Since we will no longer be giving out any cash aid, there is no need for any of those departments and agencies to have money to give out as aid.

The military, in coordination with the Advancement Department, will determine what foreign aid we can provide to allies (and other countries in times of emergencies) and coordinate which labor, education, or military services will solve the need the best.

So any country that wants something from America must determine how best to accommodate our military and our schools there.

If you're thinking right now, *But cutting off the billions of dollars we send to these countries will destabilize them and cause outbreaks of violence!*, yes, we've heard that for decades.

It always sounded like extortion to us.

If your country only exists because of American aid, you've given up your sovereignty. It's time for us to act accordingly. The preceding paragraph should have clarified that we anticipate having to help numerous countries and what that will look like (hint: expansionism).

And as for sending money like we've always done?

No. Absolutely not.

Under American Laborism, we don't pay our own citizens and legal immigrants cash benefits; we certainly don't pay a foreign country cash benefits.

Instead, we will see how we can extend our federal government to help others the same way we help our own people.

How Does This Affect Our Immigration Policy?

What you're about to read might be smeared by critics as unpopular, misconstrued, and a wedge that American Laborism detractors will attempt to use to keep Americans divided from each other.

One of the most damaging aspects of the America vs. Americans split is how it manifests in the ways our political leaders and lawmakers run the country versus what would actually be best for Americans, and, in the case of immigration, the laws already on the books. Any individual who suggests all of America's immigration laws are being followed is mistaken. That puts America in the precarious position of routinely *ignoring* laws on the books. Americans should live under laws that work well for them, not laws that are so useless most people just ignore them.

But I'm not worried about that, because by the time we finish this chapter, we'll have laid out a workable solution that addresses every critic's concerns, treats people fairly, and most importantly, extends American Laborism's benefits and establishes that it honorably stretches well beyond just lower taxes and free education.

That's right . . . you're about to solve the extremely divisive issue of whether America's resources should be used to help only citizens and legal residents, or extend even to people who are here without being born here or receiving the proper permission from our government to be a resident.

If you're not aware of it, America has an immigration system designed to welcome people from all over the world. The US Citizenship and Immigration Services (USCIS), an agency of the Department of Homeland Security, manages it.

In fact, there are many laws, regulations, and procedures in place to help people who want to become legal visitors, residents, or even citizens of America. USCIS reports that there are over 40 million legal immigrants to America, and in 2020 we welcomed over 700,000 more.[33]

These are the people who have asked our government to process their application to come here legally and have followed all the rules—even if it is just to request refugee status at a port of entry.

Of course, every one of them will be eligible for every benefit American Laborism provides . . . for life.

Does that extend to people who did not ask for permission to be here legally?

No.

Simply put: if you didn't ask for permission to be here, don't ask for federal benefits once you are here.

Unless you are a hypocrite, you have to decide if borders matter or if they don't.

If borders matter, then crossing them without permission means something. As far as the federal government under American Laborism is concerned, if a person didn't legally cross our border or ask for refugee status, they aren't legally entitled to federal assistance.

On the other hand, some people argue that borders don't matter. If that's your stance, and you therefore want to extend federal programs and benefits, do you give them to everyone?

Don't say "Yes, of course!" quite yet. Because if borders don't matter, programs and entitlements should indeed extend to everyone . . . on the entire planet.

By that argument, a few hundred million American taxpayers would be obliged to pay benefits to billions of people around the world. Or, America would be obligated to collect taxes and implement our laws globally, with no respect to, well, borders.

Do you see the paradox of saying borders don't matter when the logical step is then to extend America globally?

Is the answer then to survey each sovereign country around the world to determine which of them want to be considered borderless and, therefore, part of a borderless America—and, conversely, which countries want to defend their own borders?

This "borders mean nothing" notion is clearly absurd if you stop looking at what it means within America and begin to consider a borderless world.

But if we did entertain the idea that America's border is not a border, we must also acknowledge that anyone is welcome to cross it at will and would then be immediately eligible for benefits. We can't know how many of the world's eight billion residents would sign up for benefits, but we believe free food, clothing, shelter, and unlimited education might appeal to billions of people. With nearly two billion people living in what WorldVision.org calls "fragile contexts, characterized by impoverished conditions and dire circumstances,"[34] it's safe to assume many of them would want to sign up for our safety net if there were indeed no border restrictions.

Americans are generous, but this is impossible! It's the same as having forty people in a canoe and only seven rowing.

Don't say that's not what you meant. If you don't agree to give the same benefits to literally everyone, how do you propose we decide who gets them?

Sometimes, it seems that some people believe a border is some kind of magical one-way mirror or portal from a science fiction story. I'll wager that there are numerous people who both believe borders don't matter *and* believe that everyone within *our* borders deserves benefits—but not the rest of the world. It's a hypocritical position. If borders don't matter, you either have to treat the entire world the same or you need to, well, draw a border.

Because in reality, there isn't a one-way, magical mirror with which you can say our border should not be used to keep people out, but only people inside this border will receive our safety net.

Unfortunately, America cannot invite everyone around the world to come here, attend school, and enjoy our benefits. We simply don't have the ability to service them all here. Until we're ready to provide benefits to everyone globally—and share our laws and values—we must limit where benefits begin and end. That will be the current American border, and for all the folks who are citizens, documented immigrants, refugees, and who have a lawful right to be here.

But don't despair because American Laborism can solve the desire to help everyone.

Keep reading—we're about to completely fix the entire legal vs. illegal, documented vs. undocumented, immigrant vs. refugee problem. Plus, everyone who critiques American Laborism because we're not extending benefits to undocumented persons is dead wrong.

We've spent considerable time laying out how the Advancement Department will factor into American Laborism.

To solve this problem, we'll turn to the second department of the executive branch under Laborism: the Military Department.

First, we're going to roll DHS under the Military Department. Yes, *under*.

The military leaders will determine which aspects of DHS they still need and then integrate them. Whatever departments, agencies, or programs of the Department of Homeland Security that the military considers unnecessary or superfluous will be shut down.

Furthermore, when American Laborism critics argue that undocumented persons are entitled to full benefits in America because of how poor the conditions are in the country they came from, our military will open an investigation and determine how to best improve the conditions those people are fleeing from.

Peacefully.

Don't forget—any person in America who is undocumented here is, without exception, a citizen of another nation. Yep . . . they're documented, all right—just for somewhere else.

Therefore, from the day American Laborism is implemented, the Military Department (which will be the strongest and most well-equipped military in the world) will begin solving the problems that drive people to leave their home countries and travel to places where they are not citizens.

And America will—by working within the law—expand our global presence in as peaceful and respectful a manner as possible.

For an investment interest in the future of a country.

If it is true that there are areas where conditions are so deplorable that honest and upstanding people need to flee to America for refuge, then it's high time America comes to them. But not with handouts, and not with money that will only serve to make the leaders of said terrible place even richer.

We will help countries who both *need* and *ask for* help. Yes, it may be a bit of a balancing act to respect their sovereignty and independence while also acknowledging whatever situation they find themselves in and are unable to handle. However, with cautious and judiciously applied offers of assistance, we believe America's military and the Advancement Department can improve other countries by extending our resources and knowledge to them.

That is, by exporting American Laborism.

Let's make it clear: in no way are we proposing a costly and misguided "They'll welcome us as liberators" moment (as Vice President Dick Cheney said of the 2003 Iraq War). By responding only with in-kind aid and training to those countries so unstable that their citizens are fleeing the unsafe conditions as refugees, we should be able to avoid the mistakes of past foreign involvement and help achieve stability and a better future for people who need our help.

America—thanks to the hard work and dedication of American laborers, many of whom are immigrants—will continue to grow and prosper. We will also help people in other areas by improving their living conditions and bringing them under our control or influence.

Therefore, immigrants who have refused to seek legal status in America can return to their countries of origin and achieve the successful life they sought by leaving their homes . . . thanks to American Laborism. They'll be educated, given the opportunity to contribute labor, and our military will be on hand to ensure they're safe.

In fact, they'll be invited to work as consultants (or contractors?) with our military and Advancement Department as the first recipients of safety-net aid in the country they are citizens of, as we expand American Laborism to the places it is so clearly needed. This safety-net service, the same as we will have it in America, will be voluntary. But receiving benefits only within the country they are a citizen of—that will be a requirement.

Phil

So you said this is a program for anyone and everyone, right? Very inclusive . . . doesn't matter if you're a citizen, or even here legally. Anyone undocumented in America who needs benefits can apply, then return to their own country, where they'll receive benefits, thanks to America investigating their claim of needing help, and we send help.

Eric

I know this will be a severe hot button, because we've been allowing ourselves emotionally and intellectually to become divided on this. And to believe that we have important differences worth enough to disagree with our neighbor on—issues I don't think are as divisive as everybody thinks. I'll give you an example of this. Let's take what someone might think would be an egregious example of somebody taking advantage of the system. Perhaps that an undocumented immigrant comes across the border, shows up at a school, and says, "I'd like to participate in this school. I understand it's all free." You might as a taxpayer think, I don't want to pay for that. I don't want that person taking advantage of me paying into this Advancement Department. *Right?*

Phil

If that person you're describing asks for help and is willing to contribute and take classes, Americans would want to help them, I think. But it's fair to also say that Americans don't all want to turn on a massive electromagnet drawing two billion people here.

Eric

So now, let's work our way all the way through. That is, you have this person who could be an undocumented immigrant, who hasn't gone through the legal immigration system, hasn't agreed to follow our laws, hasn't shown any respect to our laws, may not agree with our way of life, showing up and saying, "Hey, I have labor to offer. And I'd like to be educated."

That's a tough spot to put Americans in, because we generally want to help people. And part of the undocumented immigrant debate feels like it rests on a technicality—that these may be great people and actually helping our society, but since they didn't wait their turn and let our government know who they are, they're undocumented.

So we fix this by reversing the magnet. We'll still have legal immigration and refugees, but rather than draw people to America who won't wait their turn and don't proceed legally, we'll help them in their own country by offering to take our American Laborism framework to them on a local scale.

Even those who have jaded themselves, have anger about fairness, and don't give things away in their heart —I feel like even these staunchest, most anti-immigration people might look at a system where it says this person can participate if they're, one, educating themselves and, two, offering their labor to the system to become self-sustainable . . . in their own country—that sounds like a solution.

The policy can be: "If you qualify as a refugee, apply for that status. If you want to migrate to America, apply to do so. And if you don't want to do that, if you just want a job or income or need help, don't come here outside of the legal migration, but instead ask us to come to you. We'll work with your government to bring American Laborism to you. Schools, facilities, people helping each other. We won't get in the way of charitable organizations that want to help individuals. Our part will be to help your community, so you don't need to flee." That's the only fair solution for Americans and the refugees and immigrants who are here because they followed immigration laws.

That is fairer and more in line with what you might think would be early days of America, right? When we used to challenge immigrants with the idea that you can come here, but you can't be on the public dole.

Phil

I think the wording they used was "public charge," and yes, that was made a law in the late 1800s. We've changed immigration laws over the years, though. Now, immigrants are in two categories, qualified and non-qualified. The law gets pretty complex, with lots of rules and exceptions. Suffice it to say that qualified people are generally legal immigrants and refugees, and can generally receive benefits, but some aren't eligible until they've been in America for five years. You can see that as maybe the current way we deal with making sure that some immigrants don't come to America and immediately look for benefits. And non-qualified people are generally undocumented immigrants, and they generally can't receive much in benefits.

Just to be clear, people who aren't documented and aren't legally eligible for benefits can return to where they are citizens, and we can help them there. That's offering more to undocumented people than they can expect under our current laws that give them nothing except our looking the other way and pretending they're not here.

Eric

Yeah, absolutely.

As we close this section, let's summarize what we've discussed:

- All legal immigrants and refugees to America who have our permission to be here and follow all laws are entitled to the same benefits as any other legal resident in America.

- People who are currently illegally living in America or have not gone through the proper channels to gain citizenship will not be eligible to receive any federal benefits.

- America will continue to process and respect refugee and asylum applications done legally and within the confines of the current laws we have.

- Our Advancement Department and military will actively seek opportunities to help areas around the world where people don't feel safe or suffer from economic challenges. The goal of this will be to keep people as residents of the country they are citizens of. By working closely with organizations such as Amnesty International, we can improve living conditions for people who might otherwise become refugees.

Helping People Who Speak Other Languages

The fundamental principle of American Laborism is that everyone will be treated the same, regardless of what language they speak. No benefits will be denied to anyone because they do not speak English, America's most common language—but English will remain the primary language on all our legal documents.

In addition, the federal government will do its best to accommodate every language spoken by our citizens and legal residents. However, it would have to be a fair exchange—people would also have to make every effort to speak the same language: English.

Language—something that is very personal to someone and a big part of their identity—can bring people together who share it and push people apart who do not.

Therefore, it will be an official position of American Laborism that, if you seek federal benefits, part of your obligation to participate will be to attend English-language reading and writing classes.

Of course, anyone who receives education from our safety net can take any courses or certifications they wish, but we cannot guarantee that all courses will be available in all languages, so it makes sense that improving one's English comprehension and communication skills will benefit the recipient.

It will not be presented as any effort to remove or replace non-English speakers' language, heritage, or culture. It will, however, play a role in bringing Americans together by providing them with at least a shared language.

But simultaneously, we want to reap the benefits of having different languages and cultures in America. In fact, anyone with special or bilingual language skills in America should be highly sought after for their abilities.

We know this issue carries baggage. It's our goal to respectfully weave together a family of a variety of Americans and enjoy their differences while creating common bonds.

The melting pot of America is back!

But let's return to our conversation, answering more of Phil's insightful questions.

Phil
What if someone comes from a foreign country, gets educated, and then returns home?

Eric
I get it. They participate in all this, and then they head back to their country. Doesn't that mean they've just been a beneficiary and are takers, and then they take their schooling, education, and whatever it is, and go back?

That's a price I'm willing to pay.

Phil

Wouldn't those same people export American Laborism ideals to their home country? That's sort of a good problem to have, you know?

Eric

Then that's an opportunity. How can we reach the two billion people who might want an opportunity to come here and say, "I think I'd like to live in America because of American Laborism." We bring it to them.

Phil

Solving this problem—taking care of people with needs and meeting those needs—could be attractive to a huge number of people.

Eric

Absolutely, it would. Let's take that scenario of two billion people saying, "I'd like to participate in this." If the tax base is only the tax base on the people who live, work, conduct transactions, and own something in American jurisdiction, then you could make a case for why there's no way. But if we export American Laborism, it could help two billion people.

Phil

It's interesting to think about America having that kind of positive, peaceful influence around the world. Immigrants will be asking to come here because they want to participate in American Laborism. Great, we get the American dream back. Even if they go home, great. American Laborism spreads.

Eric

Indeed. But critics will say there's no way we can afford to send help to two billion students, or they would argue that we wouldn't welcome two billion people into our schools or our military. And those certainly seem to be fair arguments.

If we're going to do this, we have to be willing to open it to everyone here who wants to participate in it. But still, how could we accommodate two billion people?

Phil

To keep it from being just a good idea that doesn't help anyone.

Eric

That means the biggest question becomes, is it sustainable? Is there any amount of sharing, laboring, participating with this that can work for everybody? An unlimited number of people? Or are we willing to believe that there are people who want to participate in this that have so little to offer that they can't? Because, OK, is this the yin and yang, and a catch-22, two sides of the coin of "these are people who may be subsistence living in other areas, and therefore American Laborism appeals to them"? Well, if they've been subsiding somewhere else, then we'll just roll out our system in their country to care for their basic needs, because that's all we're offering.

Phil

We also have to consider that economies, social structures, and other countries work on different tax scales. They also have different cultures and different levels of development. Many Third World countries would have a lot of trouble implementing this, I think.

Eric

Maybe, but we're only including the people who ask the US for *help. Maybe then an area—perhaps a country in South America or Africa—may implement this, customized differently than Scandinavia or Sri Lanka would. As you said earlier, there is a wide spectrum of people out there who will see this differently.*

What exactly we do to help them will have to be flexible, case by case, and decided as partners with each individual country. And I would imagine that if both Pakistan and sub-Saharan Africa said, "We want to roll this out," then their respective definition of meeting someone's needs might be different from ours as well as one another's.

Phil
In some cases, very different.

Eric
Does that feel at all like it would be selfish not to want to encourage basic subsystems, or a system that allows it, in other places? I don't want to fall back into the idea of, "What are we paying for this?" because in the long run, this should be self-sustainable. It shouldn't be a drain on taxes and tax money in any country.

Phil
I don't know about in terms of overpopulated areas. It's hard for me to visualize on a larger scale, in countries so different from America.

Eric
That may be a challenge for this, because the world is a big place with cultural differences, and you have to respect that. America has always been the melting pot that has absorbed other valuable contributors to our society. There's no question that many of the

people who will come *and* have come *to America over the past two hundred years or more have participated to make it better. No question at all, right?*

Phil
Yeah.

Eric
But can we get an idea like this to go global and change the lives of billions of people? Or are Americans that different from other people? I know it will work here, but I don't know about other places. What's the solution? Is there a solution that we would say we'd like to help with this? You know, we'll make it available for people to participate in their own country?

Is there an opportunity to transition other societies over and help build their own version of it? Or will time tell us that this is a uniquely American opportunity, the mixture of capitalists wanting to be left alone and safety-net people needing to be taken care of, yet given an opportunity to excel . . . to climb up the ladder of independence and eventual success?

Is that uniquely American? I don't think so. I think there are probably many people around the world who would want this.

Phil
Then the question becomes, where is the line between "That's not uniquely American" and "It may also not be for everyone"? That's fair because democracy hasn't been absorbed everywhere around the world, right? And economic systems are different for different people.

CHAPTER 13

MIDDLE-CLASS FAMILIES, THEIR HEALTHCARE, AND AMERICAN LABORISM

Phil

So, looking at it from more of an opposition point of view here, when you're dealing with people who would sign up for these federal government programs, we're not talking about somebody who is a billionaire or well enough off that they can handle themselves, right? You are talking about someone who is probably lower-income, if they're going to provide a service and can't be compensated for it, correct?

Eric

Yes. I would imagine so.

Phil

If they're not lifers, and they're doing it so they can not only better themselves but also better provide back to the community, are they going to get crushed in the private sector if they ever try to compete with somebody from Harvard, for example? Can people educated in a government-funded school actually compete with the graduates of other schools?

Eric

That is a real concern that people will have to determine. Do I want to spend hundreds of thousands of dollars for a Harvard education, or does it make sense for me to take free schooling? Our plan puts that "not wealthy" student in a better position, in my opinion, because they have always competed against elite school grads. That won't change, but you have the option of staying out of debt when you do it.

Phil

Another concern is, we're talking about getting rid of federal government loans and federal government money for school at a college level, right?

Eric

Yes.

Phil

Let's take a pre-American Laborism look at most schools that average, middle-class people attend—state schools or even private colleges. Assuming the student isn't on a full-ride scholarship and these aren't federal schools, the kids that are going are compensating the school with federal funding, loans, and grants, right?

Eric

You're saying the school today isn't a government school, but because the kids might pay their tuition with grants or federally insured loans, the government has something to do with the school's funding? Then, yes.

Phil

So my question is, will the federal government directly fund participating American Laborism schools? Or are the kids going to get the money to go to school with the services provided? How does that work exactly? Is it a voucher system?

Eric

A drastic oversimplification would be to imagine two kinds of schools. And again, it seems like we're focusing on college and college kids, which is certainly a big worry for middle-class parents, but not the only worry. They also want their younger children to have access to good schools.

Phil

True. And dont forget older people wanting free education for career advancement or even to retool themselves or pursue something new.

Eric

Excellent point. But we can still say middle-class families would decide between two kinds of schools. Let's call them Laborism schools *and* participating schools. *Both include anything from pre-K to advanced degrees, vocational or technical, or even simply, language schools.*

The difference is, Laborism schools are built from the ground up, knowing they're part of the system. They are perfectly in tune with people working one day and signing up for at least a day's worth of classes. All their funding comes from our taxes, and they strive to get the labor contributions to cover as much of what the school needs as possible.

Participating schools are the schools that weren't built for this. They already have a student body that is paying tuition to attend.

Phil

Those—the participating schools—that's my question. How do they get paid for enrolling someone who is signing up for free education?

Here's why I'm asking: There are several examples of for-profit schools cheating to get paid by the government. I don't want middle-class families paying their taxes and trusting the government, only to have these schools ripping them off. It's happened before. A lot.

Eric

Then the system has to be something that can't be gamed.

Phil

Absolutely. But we want the existing schools to be participating schools—just not gaming the system with fake attendees.

Eric

I wanted to talk about this—specifically payments, and how it's possible—a little later. I'll say I see it as something you'll like, and it won't waste a penny of middle-class taxpayers' money.

> *For now, I'll just say the Advancement Department weaves together blockchain for tracking payments and AI for tracking lesson plans, student progress, making sure the payments match the students, and the students are real people.*

Phil

You're right . . . I like that. Train the same AI that's helping the students to watch for fraud patterns. No fake students. People pay their taxes, the taxes pay the schools, and blockchain gives visibility. This will be great for the middle class who want their money's worth.

Defining the middle class in America is harder than you might think. Turns out, *middle class* is one of those concepts that everyone knows, but no one can precisely pin down who and how many people make up the middle class. There's even a Brookings.edu website that compares twelve different definitions of the middle class.[35]

The result? Those dozen definitions range from 10 percent to 71 percent of the population being in the middle class. Read that carefully, as it says there may be thirty-three million folks in the American middle class . . . or there could be *seven times* that many.

The reason that defining the middle class is so challenging is because there's remarkable diversity among this group. We're not just talking about splitting the group into upper- and lower-middle class, either. There are middle-class people who work trades, serve as lower management, are semi-professionals and run small businesses, as well as highly educated people who work as managers and salaried professionals.

Perhaps one reason accuracy is difficult when determining how many people are in the middle class is because social scientists often focus on standard of living. But that in itself is hard to define. Sure, we can calculate that the median household income in America was $69,021[36] according to the 2020 US census, but what does that tell us?

Could someone earning less than $69,000 but living in an area with a low cost of living have the same standard of living as someone who earns more than $69,000 and lives somewhere with a high cost of living?

Interestingly, the census also takes into account your family size when calculating median income and does so across all fifty states, plus Washington, DC, Guam, Northern Marianas Islands, Puerto Rico, and the Virgin Islands.[37] What it shows is that a family of four in Puerto Rico is "median" at the same income as a single person living in Washington, DC.

So basing middle-class membership purely on income and family size doesn't work. You know what does? College education, according to the National Center for Education Statistics (NCES). In May 2023, the NCES published a study of full-time, year-round workers aged 25–35, which found that "higher educational attainment was associated with higher median earnings."[38]

However, it's also true that in 2020, the Federal Reserve Bank of Cleveland published a report titled "Is the Middle Class Worse Off Than It Used to Be?" in which they found that education prices grew over 600 percent more than incomes.[39]

That means even as median incomes rose, the price of education rose 600 percent *faster*.

If education is what's necessary to increase your income, but the price of education is growing faster than incomes—by a large margin—do you need to hear anything else about how American Laborism's free, unlimited, lifetime education is possibly the best benefit any American could ever ask for?

Remember, asking for help under American Laborism and participating in receiving your free education isn't a full-time job or an all-or-nothing proposal. With requirements of a day of school and a day of labor contribution, you can easily still work and care for your family.

American Laborism doesn't leave out the American middle class. In fact, they'll get a lot out of it. The Cleveland Fed study that we referenced also found that healthcare prices rose over 200 percent more than incomes, making education and healthcare the two biggest costs of the middle class that are rising faster than income can keep up with. Because of that, we'll later look briefly at how runaway healthcare costs with diminishing services might be affected by American Laborism and what we'd do about healthcare costs if we could.

Can People with Children Benefit from American Laborism?

Phil
What about people with children? Having children does not prevent them from going to school or continuing their education. Some people even work to support their children while continuing their education. But there are also people for whom it might not be possible to do both—raise their kids and continue or finish their education. What do we do about them?

Eric

Oh, for sure, there are people who have taken a year or two of college, or maybe only finished high school, or perhaps didn't finish high school. There might be someone with a degree who wants more education. Or they work for themselves and want more skills. For other people, perhaps school has always been a struggle, but they want to try. All these different people can further their education.

Phil

Right, because obviously education is available for anyone who wants it.

Eric

Yes, no exceptions. This might be the most straightforward example of the value of contributing the day of labor. We'll be matching people's skills with the different needs we'll have in/through the Advancement Department, right? Well, one of the skills many of these people will have is the ability to take care of children. I'm probably oversimplifying this, but why can't parents who want to attend classes keep one another's kids in a special daycare facility? It's essentially a mass babysitting trade, but one that enables all the interested parents time and freedom to pursue their education.

Phil

But wouldn't that mean people trusting their children with someone who may or may not be good with children? That's a lot of trust in strangers, right?

Eric

Here we are again with super-specific logistics. The schools would have requirements for people who want to participate by

*contributing their labor toward childcare. Of course, there would
have to be some requirements on that. Clearly, you can't have
someone get thirty kids dropped on them on day one.*

Phil
*It makes sense that whatever state they live in, they'd need to meet
that state's guidelines or restrictions for childcare, and if they don't
meet those, and assuming there's no legal reason that an individual can't care for children, then they could start helping the
people who are licensed, and the first thing they take on as their
educational benefit is whatever is needed to get licensed, certified,
or approved in their state.*

Eric
It's fun to think about this logistically, rather than theoretically.

Phil
Theoretically, as in, this is a good idea, *and logistically,* as in,
here is how we make it work?

Eric
*Yes, because within this system of Advancement Department safe-
ty-net schools, there will be a wide spectrum of participants and
skills and needs. How exciting to think of all the different people
who come for help and have help to offer.*

*And I hope the biggest problem is balancing these out to
where everybody's taking care of one another.*

American Laborism will be great for families with children.
Much better, in fact, than how America seems to have enacted policies as if our political leaders are surprised to learn that families exist.

It could be said that, sadly, America is working against the

interests of Americans in this particular instance, and the ramifications are obviously and painfully clear.

But we're solving two problems for families—that of America's
inadequate benefits programs that virtually never help the middle
class and underperforming and dangerous schools that many middle-
class families are unable to escape from.

The subject has been studied deeply, and this book is
intended as a forward-looking guide, so we won't spend too much
time rehashing what *doesn't* work. But suffice it to say, we believe
American Laborism is correcting a massive tragedy that has punished
and held Americans back while claiming to be helping them: that
is, the gaming of safety-net benefits. By *gaming*, we mean when the
rules for something allow for an unexpected, unfair, or even morally
unacceptable outcome. We'll give you an example, and we'll try to
stay away from political hot-buttons.

Let's say a gas station wants to run a promotion that says if you
buy your gas from them, you get an ice cream cone "for the children
in the car." Clearly, the promotion's intention is to get you to visit
the station and fill your tank, and the ice cream cone is meant to
be a small incentive. But you can be sure there are some folks who
note the promotion doesn't require a minimum amount of gas or a
maximum number of kids. Uh-oh.

Gaming the system here could mean a school bus pulling in,
buying a penny's worth of gas, and driving off with dozens of children enjoying their "free" ice cream. Did the bus driver technically
break the terms of the free ice-cream offer? No. But did they find
a loophole to maximize their benefit (while minimizing the gas
station's)? Absolutely.

Figuring out how to offer quality benefits while structuring
them to avoid gaming is a decades-long problem. Benefits have been
rolled out and then rolled back, increased and then decreased, nego-
tiated by wealthy and out-of-touch politicians who've likely never

worried about feeding their children, and debated by Supreme Court justices who literally are guaranteed employment for life.

And through all that, while trying to best manage our benefit programs, it's rare that benefits are ever extended to middle-class, median-income families. Certainly, no free, unlimited lifetime education has ever been offered to middle-class families.

But with American Laborism, they can be, because, of course, children have basic needs that need to be met. As long as a family with children wants to participate, they are welcome.

Suffice it to say that the benefits American Laborism provides will be unlimited for families the same as for individuals. And the reasonable requirements for contributing some labor and attending appropriate classes still apply.

Here's how that works: The educational facilities will determine the level of schooling appropriate for each child exactly the way they do for every adult. For most children, nothing will change. America and each state already have education laws that determine what age children need to attend school, which is most often paid for by the state or municipality they live in.

For many families with children, this will solve a massive problem: underperforming schools they would have otherwise been forced to send their kids to, which often plagues low-income and middle-class families. That's because while it's possible that some private and charter schools will want to participate in the Advancement Department's free and unlimited lifetime education, there's no guarantee they will. There's also no guarantee that every neighborhood will have top-performing schools or even a choice of schools to attend.

Until now.

Education is so important that we will provide free and unlimited education to every person who wants it, even if they could attend a local, city, or state pre-kindergarten, elementary, middle, or high school. Yes, every child in every family who wants the best education available is eligible for Advancement Department–provided schooling. Someone in the family will need to meet the labor contribution requirements—but nobody will have to attend an underperforming or even dangerous school anymore. (Hopefully, you've read how we plan to integrate AI into lesson planning and use the best practices available to deliver top-notch education to everyone. That applies to children too!)

And as for the labor contribution of the children, that will be determined by the parents and, as we said, the applicable laws. American Laborism believes in labor, but not illegal child labor!

The advantage of providing benefits that are not cash, income, or means-tested is that people have no opportunity to game the system.

Families with children will receive the benefits they need and contribute a reasonable amount of their labor, while receiving the best free and unlimited education.

We're confident families will love it.

How This Helps Families Caring for People Living with Disabilities

Now, what about families that include people with disabilities?

This is complicated, of course. We believe it is natural for everyone in a society to want to take care of those among us who face greater-than-average challenges and/or cannot take care of themselves.

At the same time, many of us are also aware of cases where a program created with good intentions failed to adequately meet the needs of these same people.

Some people need more resources than others to live their best life possible, and this is something we need to consider. And many of those people rely on their family to help. It can be a financial, emotional, and time burden on the family.

There is no doubt that solving this need to help people who require extra resources and the families who care for them will be a challenge for American Laborism too.

Here's how we'll tackle this:

First, be assured that folks with greater needs will always get their needs met if they ask the federal government for help. Remember, literally every individual is equal under American Laborism and deserves to be treated equally. That may mean a greater amount of the labor contributions of others may be directed to the care of a very small minority of people with greater needs.

But we'll remind you that just a few pages ago, when we discussed that everyone would be contributing, you could have made the argument that it was hard to see how we'd find something for millions of people to do.

Or you might have wondered about someone pursuing an advanced degree in medicine, physical therapy, or hospitality, for example—what kind of labor would they be expected to contribute?

Second, we would correctly match the folks with valuable skills to where they can help people with the greatest challenges, even if it's just by offering support to the families already doing the job of taking care of someone who needs extra care.

Third, while this is happening, we would anticipate future improvements to the entire system that will only be possible— and, frankly, revealed—by our entire society operating at the higher level of everyone being as fully educated as possible and having their basic needs met. If we aren't going to allow ourselves to hope that solutions we haven't thought of yet will present themselves, and therefore these great challenges will be solved, then we need to start now.

Sure, hope is not a strategy. We know that.

But covering everyone's basic needs, so the entire community can contribute, and anyone who wishes can receive unlimited education and, presumably, apply some of this toward our greatest challenges—that is a strategy.

It's the strategy of "educating the daylights out of whoever wants it, and then turning them loose on solving problems."

Can We Protect Middle-Class Families from Labor-Saving Devices and Technologies?

This is American *Labor*ism. We believe labor has value. It should surprise no one that we're not enthusiastic about labor-saving devices—and often labor-saving devices cause our communities to no longer need the labor of folks working their way up through the layers of the middle class.

Maybe it's worth being more specific. Of course, clearing the snow off your sidewalk would be more labor-intensive if you didn't use a shovel, so by that logic a shovel is a labor-saving device. We're not talking about that.

We're more talking about machines, robots, and processes that, for example, when deployed, can put people out of work. And obviously, people who are out of work not only find their lives changed, but also often turn to the federal government for benefits.

At the same time, however, we have to address the real fact that often labor-saving devices are invented to solve either excessive costs of labor or lack of suitable human workers for dangerous, mundane, or repetitive jobs. Some of those jobs cause injury to the humans who do them, and replacing humans at risk with robots therefore can't just be seen as a one-sided argument.

Not to mention cost. Let's say that the only person who could do a particular job demanded a $1,000 hourly wage. That might be a good time to look into AI or robotics if you wanted to increase your profits or lower your costs to your customers. Another two-sided argument.

Earlier, we talked about the possibility that artificial intelligence and robotics could disrupt America's workforce. Since we've already covered that, we'll just answer here what we'll do—as much as possible—to protect as much upward mobility among the middle class. We'll disallow any kind of tax deduction, in any fashion—expense, depreciation, write-offs—that will provide zero benefit in the tax code.

To put it simply, companies won't be able to reduce their federal taxes by investing in and depreciating a device or technology that saves labor.

But we also understand that labor-saving devices and technologies can make companies more competitive, which could mean more sales and more profits, which could mean more tax revenue. So looking ahead optimistically, we'll plant the seed that perhaps this tax policy can be waived in times of full-labor participation, and perhaps even revisit the policy once the federal debt is paid off.

But these moves may not be enough to counter the argument that focusing on labor might stifle innovation. That brings up the question of whether it is our intention to limit innovation or perhaps freeze it just to protect labor? The answer is no, we do not intend to stifle innovation, and in fact, we don't even see a lack of innovation as an unintended side effect of American Laborism. Nor do we intend to just stuff people into meaningless jobs purely for the satisfaction of having them contribute labor. We must find the right balance between supporting labor and allowing innovation, even among those seeking to acquire and grow their capital.

We're confident that America can do this, and history gives us a great example. Adam Smith's *The Wealth of Nations* was first published in 1776. This book, often cited as an economic foundation for capitalism, is exactly as old as America, which capitalism certainly helped to build. Capitalism was first implemented in a time of blacksmiths, horseback travel, merchants shipping gold, tea, spices, and raw materials, and parchment treaties signed with quill pens.

After two and a half centuries of focusing on capital accumulation, capitalism has traded in iron horseshoes and trade winds for collateralized debt obligations, synthetic financial instruments, syndicated loans, banks with no reserves, global stock exchanges, and billion-dollar transactions with counterparties on the other side of the globe, betting on the direction interest rates will take. Capitalism, thanks to our yearning to maximize the value of capital, has innovated.

So, a critic of American Laborism may see our work requirement as risking creating so-called make-work placeholder or dead-end jobs. Remember, the most well-known example of make-work in America was President Franklin Roosevelt's job-boosting Public Works Administration and the Works Progress Administration, which yielded us the Hoover Dam, New York City's Robert F. Kennedy Bridge, and the San Antonio River Walk in Texas. But there's more to Laborism, and it's why we're retooling the Department of Education as Advancement Department. The expectation is that by pairing educational advancement with work, even those with mundane jobs today can find themselves advancing into more fulfilling jobs in the future rather than staying put simply by asking to advance themselves and providing a small amount of their labor. Plus, remember, the American Laborism work commitment is one day a week, not full-time, and only for those seeking benefits.

Of course, there will always be companies wanting to innovate to make the best product at the lowest cost. And some of those might seek out ways to reduce their labor costs. American Laborism won't prevent them from using labor-saving technologies. But we also won't let them deduct the cost from their taxes. It simply means that labor-saving technologies must pay for themselves because the cost won't be shared with other taxpayers. We think that's fair.

What about Healthcare?

Right now, more than 35,000 American homes are in foreclosure.[40] In 2022, nearly 400,000 people declared bankruptcy in America.[41] Each year, between 1.5 and 1.8 million cars are repossessed in America due to nonpayment.[42] And according to the US Federal Reserve, as many as 24.5 million credit cards are delinquent their payments right now.[43]

We love America and Americans, but looking at these statistics, we have to state the obvious: Americans sometimes obligate themselves to payments they simply can't afford to make.

The way we pay for healthcare is one of them, and it's taking a lot of money from the middle class.

Healthcare, or more precisely, healthcare benefits, is a controversial topic, to say the least. That's an important distinction, because while most people agree Americans should have access to world-class healthcare, few of us agree how much it should cost us to access it, and how much of it should be a benefit paid for by our neighbors.

Yes, that's right, it's not some nameless, faceless government that generously pays for benefits; it's other Americans—our friends and neighbors—who pay for all benefits in America at this time. (And because we're more than $32 trillion in debt and rising, some taxpayers whom we expect to pay for our benefits may not have even been born yet! If you like generous benefits, thank the next infant you see—they're paying for them!)

But if we're trying to reduce the size of government—even eliminating numerous departments, including Health and Human Services—how does healthcare, which is 18.3 percent of our economy,[44] fit in?

Are we proposing to simply cancel all federal government involvement with healthcare completely?

The answer is no . . . but we have some improvements to make that could help prevent healthcare from bankrupting us. (That's not hyperbole, either. CNBC reported 66.5 percent of US personal bankruptcies were due to medical issues—either high costs for care or time off work[45]—and paradoxically, the *Washington Post* reported that personal bankruptcies due to medical expenses are actually *increasing* since America passed the Affordable Care Act.)[46]

It's not just personal bankruptcies, either. A study by the OECD warned that "health care is growing as a share of the economy and government budgets in ways that appear unsustainable."[47]

But changing or improving healthcare and healthcare coverage in America presents a challenge because we want the best possible coverage, but we also want it to be affordable. Some people even want it to be free. We want to be healthy, enjoying low deductibles, copays, and premiums, but we don't eat less and exercise more. We want doctors and healthcare professionals to be attentive and spend the time to get to know us without rushing, but we don't like waiting for them when their other appointments run long. We want access to the best procedures, therapies, and medicines benefiting from years, if not decades, of research, but we don't want big corporations making big profits from our ills. We want trim waistlines, but still want to eat the large supreme pizza.

Healthcare is nearly one-fifth of our national economy, getting more expensive at an unsustainable rate, responsible for far too many personal bankruptcies, and apparently a tangled heap of unsolvable paradoxes.

That's the mess we're in now.

But that's not what the future has to look like, and American Laborism holds the key. It's important to understand that, just like America itself is made up of an uncountable variety of peoples and cultures with varied habits and diets, so is the variety of health-care problems our overworked healthcare system faces. Some of us overeat. Some consume too much alcohol. Some smoke. Some exercise . . . and some don't. Others may take vitamins and supplements, while others overlook taking any medication. Some of us work in dangerous jobs or partake in risky activities, and some are even exposed to toxins or carcinogens where we live, work, or go to school.

It would be unrealistic (and impossible) for us to claim that American Laborism can solve every health challenge Americans face.

But there are three we can immediately improve—and they pay big dividends. We also have another secret weapon that will help us and a sure-fire strategy to at least get the costs of healthcare under control.

First, by making sure anyone who asks for benefits gets proper nutrition, we can improve the immediate and long-term health of both adults and children suffering from undernutrition. Just eating better can reduce heart disease, diabetes, and obesity over the long-term—all of which decrease your health and increase how much healthcare you need.

Second, we can task our educators to provide better information about nutrition and make it part of mandatory classes that everyone seeking benefits needs to take. You likely already understand how food choices can affect your overall health. But some people may not already know that, and if we can improve their health by educating them on the benefits of eating better and the costs of poor eating habits, then it's worth pursuing.

Third, we're going to roll out an American exercise plan. Fitness, exercise, and personal discipline experts from the military will work with school coaches and kinesiology experts to develop exercise plans that will help all Americans get into shape. Of course, we know nobody can force Americans to get into shape, and virtually every prior effort to do this has failed. But this time, we can't allow ourselves to fail. We must develop a community desire to participate in this for our own health. We can even make fun challenges, such as "walk your neighborhood with your mail carrier" and "run with the soldiers," or even obstacle courses.

If this sounds silly or even whimsical to you, consider the alternative: a wealthy country with an underperforming and and overwhelmed healthcare system that eats up nearly a fifth of every dollar every American worker and every American company produces year in and year out.

As far as the collective health of Americans goes, we're not just talking about helping the folks asking for benefits to get healthy; we want our health programs to make the whole country healthier.

But for the small portion of America who are asking for benefits, we have a secret weapon that will benefit them health-wise. And that is the inverse correlation between level of education and obesity. Simply put, the lower your education level in America, the more likely you are to be obese. And the higher your education level, the less likely you are to be obese.

That sounds fantastic for an American economic structure that encourages education. In 2011, Professor Jay Bhattacharya of Stanford University School of Medicine and Professor Neeraj Sood of Schaeffer Center for Health Policy and Economics published research that showed that while obesity in Americans was growing overall, it was consistently lower among more educated people.[48]

We don't know if it's possible to reverse obesity by increasing education, because we're not aware of that ever being studied. But it's clear that increasing education before someone becomes obese could be a factor in reducing overall obesity, which will reduce heart disease and diabetes, in turn helping the overburdened American healthcare system.

This is just the beginning of the improvements American Laborism offers.

By restructuring where community healthcare decisions are made and how the "affordable" care coverage is paid for, we can make even more improvements, especially at the federal level. It's important to remember the capacity in which federal healthcare should be administered under the blanket of American Laborism. We are talking about a safety-net level of coverage. The federal government currently provides healthcare coverage such as Medicare, Medi-Cal, Veterans' Health Administration, Indian Health Service, DOD Tricare, and the State Children's Health Insurance Program.[49]

Obamacare was introduced to allow healthcare coverage to reach millions of people who may not otherwise be able to afford it. It was considered a reform of the previous system, but not without its flaws and severe inefficiencies. People were sold on the idea that "everyone" would have coverage even if it was free due to lack of income. But as we all know, nothing is truly free without consequence. Numerous studies from organizations ranging from *Forbes* to the Brookings Institute to the University of Pennsylvania conducted in the first decade after the Affordable Care Act was passed show that health costs for Americans *rose* after its passage, are currently more expensive than ever before, and continue to rise.

Not only has healthcare become more expensive with increased monthly premiums, out-of-pocket maximums, or the plethora of indecipherable charges on the explanation of benefits—aka "bill"—that you are too overwhelmed to follow up on with your insurance company because you're already counting how many buttons you have to press in their automated system to reach a real person. Either that or having to repeat "representative" countless times until you wonder which one of you is actually the robot.

But we're not here simply to complain about the inefficiencies of our current system. We've already mentioned a workable plan to achieve a healthier society—which Americans obviously have the freedom to ignore if they want to. Nobody can force Americans to get healthier; we can just make it easy and attractive for them.

But we can make some policy changes that, if implemented, will improve the overall healthcare system.

Phil and I tried to talk our way through this convoluted and confusing challenge. We'll share some of our conversation to give you a glimpse of the sincere effort we're making to solve the challenge of how much healthcare benefits America wants to be on the hook for.

Phil

What about healthcare? As far as the federal government goes, that is.

Eric

It should be sent completely to the states. It's sort of a quasi-national plan confusingly managed by the federal government and states. I'd love to see it 100 percent pushed to the states and taken out of federal hands entirely.

Phil

I'm pretty sure the Affordable Care Act prohibits that. But OK, say it's possible, and pushing it back to the states survives legal challenges. Why would you want to shift healthcare to the states?

Eric

Two reasons. First, localization or regionalization. Because Washington State spends a third as much on healthcare as Virginia does.

Second reason, because the federal government can use deficit and debt to pay for healthcare. It's selfish, inefficient, and unsustainable.

Now, eliminate the possibility of hiding the costs of the so-called Affordable Care Act in bloated budgets, even the exact same plan but administered by the states, without deficits or debt . . . and those plans will have to live within a budget.

Phil

We're somewhat in the opposite of that right now, aren't we? States create plans and markets if they want, joining the federal plan if they want, but yes, the money is obscured.

But I still don't think any dramatic changes are legally possible.

Eric

I have a plan for that contingency.

I fully expect the minute we say the entire executive branch is military, schools, and post office, there will be people demanding that they have a brand-new constitutional right to the government meeting all their healthcare needs.

Phil

Safe bet. Some people already want that.

Eric

There's no arguing that the ACA does not offer everything to everyone. But there will be people who exaggerate how important a program it is, without ever addressing how expensive and inefficient it is.

If we can't make it legal to push it to the states to put on their budgets and their tax base, giving frugal and healthy states the ability to lower healthcare costs, here's what we do:

Separate the tax for ACA out, track every penny of it using public blockchain ledgers—obviously with privacy of our personal data—and remove it from withholding and payroll taxes of any kind. Let's go all the way. If it's a great program, we'll bill people honestly and individually.

American Laborism tax will be 10 percent income tax plus 0.25 percent wealth tax. The entire government except for healthcare will run on that.

Affordable Care Act tax will probably be something like 20–25 percent, I'm guessing.

Phil

People will hate that.

Eric

For about a year.

Because the small number of people who would scream if we tried to move healthcare entirely to the states will be drowned out by the huge crowd who will explode if we make them write a check for the full cost of ACA. And since the Supreme Court has found Obamacare is a tax, we shouldn't have any trouble from courts or lawmakers asking people to pay the tax that our lawmakers voted in for us.

So here we go: every month you send us 25 percent of your income, and we'll leave the ACA alone. Six months in, we'll have people wondering why it's so expensive if their deductible is still thousands of dollars.

Twelve months in, we'll have people demanding change. Maybe someone will say, "How can we have a national health-care plan without a national exercise plan? A national diet? A national no-smoking goal? A national stop drinking campaign?"

Phil

It wouldn't be long before people realize the amount of healthcare people think they need is not the same if they have to pay for all those bloated inefficiencies out of their own pocket month in and month out.

This could change the momentum in America and the world toward asking for healthcare that can't possibly be delivered, and while you're at it, asking for free or low-cost and high-perfor-mance healthcare.

Eric

I don't think that's something fair to the citizens or taxpayers—the notion that you can have top-notch, low-cost, all-your-ques-tions-answered, all-your-needs-met healthcare. I just don't think that's possible. And I think anybody who's been trying to gather votes, trying to gather political power by pretending that that's possible, has been lying to America.

Phil

It sounds like you're saying it's going to fall on us—on American Laborism—to tell people the truth that the current state of healthcare in America is more expensive than one might believe something called the Affordable Care Act would be. Healthcare benefits, and the costs to pay them, are part of the government spending that is bankrupting America. This is a real America vs. Americans situation. We're paying billions for something that a recent Gallup poll said less than half of Americans rate positively.[50]

Eric

But I also believe people have healthcare needs.

I guess the easiest way for me to understand this is every-body who's a capitalist will feel like they're getting something out of this and losing something. Everybody who expects the federal government to completely take over healthcare may feel like they're giving something up in this, but it's a trade-off that we now meet every other basic need and get rid of the unfairness of capitalism, so to speak.

And that means we may have to dial back what part of healthcare we feel is the federal government's responsibility, because you can argue that no part of healthcare is the federal government's responsibility, right?

But healthcare will be difficult. Healthcare is probably the largest, most misunderstood ox to get gored in this, because I believe there are many false sales jobs going on with this. I believe we've been hoodwinked to believe that the federal government can meet all our healthcare needs with a reasonable budget. I think that's impossible. So what we're presenting is that we'll give up something that is impossible to obtain, and then we'll replace it with something that is possible to obtain and localize it.

Absolutely, the states will have to take this on. So if there's something that a state believes it wants to attempt to have social- ized medicine, the state can attempt to provide it. But anybody who bristles at that idea probably thinks, Well, I'm in a small state, *or* I'm in a state that doesn't earn as much. *And what they were hoping for was that wealthy people in other states would pay for their healthcare.*

The federal government has become so monolithic that what's also happened is it's now separate from the people. It's this layer of bureaucracy that filters people from one another. If I stopped a random stranger on the street and asked, "Don't you agree that the federal government should pay for [fill in the blank]?," they'd probably say yes. But if I asked them to person- ally donate to it, they probably wouldn't. It's easier to spend "the government's" money than our own. The problem is, the govern- ment doesn't have any money of its own. All the government's money is our *money, collected through taxes.*

If you're someone who believes your healthcare should be paid for by the government, you cannot ignore the fact that the money they use for that comes from your neighbor. But would you ever go to your neighbor personally and demand that they pay your hospital bill? Of course not! Yet we don't think about that when we talk about government-controlled healthcare.

We're no longer in a position where, if we want something, we ask our community for it. But we're literally doing that when we expect the government to pay for something.

We're just asking a middleman to do that for us.

And we've allowed ourselves to become comfortable with this, which works against our own interests.

CHAPTER 14

HOW WILL ANY OF THIS BE POSSIBLE?

HOW CAN WE DO THIS?

The short answer is *blockchain* and *American innovation*.

This is not only possible, but it will actually be easy and will provide a better level of service for everyone who wants to participate than they have ever enjoyed from their government services.

Here's what we need to do: make sure everyone who asks for help receives it. We have explained this in previous chapters.

But we must also keep track of the benefits, recipients, and taxes that everyone pays.

We get it—no one likes to be tracked. Read on, though. You will love what we do here.

First of all, we need to decide what we are willing to accept as the facts of where we are at the moment, assuming we do nothing.

There are two possibilities.

First, that our government is *already able* to track the tax money we send to them, as well as where it goes, what it is spent on, and who ultimately receives it. If this is true, then all the money is tracked, but the information just isn't shared with us. Which is baloney, because it's our money.

The only other possibility is that the government is *unable* to track who makes their tax payments, where the money goes, and ultimately who ends up with it.

If that is the case, we should be beyond outraged. Seriously, why pay taxes if the money cannot be tracked?

We believe our government is fully capable of tracking money. But they choose not to tell us where it goes, except to provide questionable reports, budgets, and logs of expenditures. Then they move some of our money in such a way that tracking it becomes difficult or impossible . . . intentionally.

Unfortunately, we are at a time when the citizens of our country are over $32 trillion in debt and have very little to show for it.

American Laborism is our only chance to change this. And we'll do it by initiating a program that allows every dollar that moves through the federal government to be tracked, down to the penny.

Literally *every* penny.

Now, granted, we understand that some of that money has a plausible argument for privacy. Salaries for folks working for the government are a perfect example. We will not make public the salaries of individual employees.

The good news is that blockchain uniquely can solve the problem of making every penny trackable while maintaining privacy in the cases that it is appropriate. This might blow your mind, but what would you think about turning the tables on our government and giving ourselves a currency that allows *us* to track *their* spending but doesn't allow *them* to track *ours*?

Even better news—some blockchain technologies that make this possible are being developed right here in America!

If you're unfamiliar with blockchain and decentralized ledger technology, or if you're somewhat familiar yet unsure of the benefits, we'd like for you to consider the benefits of blockchain versus the alternative of not changing anything.

Consider this: most blockchains accurately trace transactions all the way back to the moment they launched. For bitcoin, for example, every transaction that ever happened on the bitcoin network (even those worth less than a millionth of a cent!) can be quickly traced back to January 3, 2009, the day the world's most popular cryptocurrency launched its blockchain.

Don't you wish you could trace every penny the government spent since 2009? We sure do.

We're not suggesting the US government start using the bitcoin network and cryptocurrency for all its payments. We are saying that the blockchain technology that makes bitcoins' accuracy possible should be used.

So yes, we expect a legitimate transition period to bring the United States government up to speed. But we also don't expect it to be more than one year. When we implement American Laborism, we will therefore integrate a one-year deadline such that after that date, any government payment that is not trackable down to the penny will not be valid.

And with that, we solve many problems all in twelve months.

As satisfying as it would be to have visibility into everything the federal government spends money on, that's only part of making American Laborism work. Innovation is more than just following the money.

Therefore, as we near the end of our introduction to American Laborism, we'll leave you with five concepts that can take American Laborism from idea to reality. They are:

1. Deploy blockchain and decentralized ledger technology.
2. Utilize American innovation (AI and others).
3. Return to an asset-backed currency.
4. Build more schools.
5. Build more housing.

Let's address each concept individually.

CONCEPT 1: Deploy Blockchain and Decentralized Ledger Technology

As we've mentioned, blockchain technology offers fantastic benefits when it comes to accurately keeping track of something. We described how every penny the government spends could be tracked if we used blockchain to do it.

But we can also use the technology to ensure that every student gets every benefit they deserve. Plus, every school and employer can immediately audit and account for every student they are helping or employing, keeping budgets 100 percent accurate and up to date. And we can do all this while maintaining the privacy of everyone receiving benefits.

If you're not familiar with blockchain or the other phrase we have been using—*decentralized ledger technology*—it's OK. You don't need to be. For now, think of blockchain as a database or spreadsheet, or even a checkbook register that tracks information. Simply put, it can be accessible for anyone to review while remaining safe from them changing it (even hackers). There are even blockchains that can protect against the future threat of quantum computers.

But blockchain can do more than just protect data while sharing it; it can also verify identities without compromising an individual's privacy. Furthermore, it can verify balances without telling anyone how much money you have. It can also be set up to automatically pay a paycheck when it's due or turn on a heater when the temperature dips—all without handing over the control of your account or your thermostat to anyone else. People, companies, and countries are using blockchain for currency transactions, tracking supply chains and fighting counterfeiting, and guaranteeing that medicines given to people are safe. Blockchains' decentralized finance has even created exchanges with no counterparty and asset-backed loans that pay themselves off.

In other words, using blockchain to finally get visibility into our government spending won't be difficult for this technology.

I should note that I (Eric) have been researching blockchain since 2013. I've invested in various cryptocurrencies and mined many of them myself using powerful computers. Over the past five-and-a-half years, I've published enough research on different cryptocurrencies to fill four more books. I'm keeping this section intentionally short, though, because I don't want the acceptance of American Laborism to be perceived as primarily about blockchain.

CONCEPT 2: Utilize American Innovation

In previous chapters, we described the coming innovation and disruption that artificial intelligence will bring. By harnessing AI, we'll be able to mitigate virtually all the possible disruption that American workers feel.

AI can be used to retrain displaced workers. It can create lessons for students of all education levels. It can also look for patterns to detect opportunities for improvement as well as sniff out fraud and people gaming the system.

We're integrating AI because its capabilities of analyzing vast amounts of information can customize education for every individual. That's just one area we're innovators in, however, because America has a rich culture of innovation that has driven the country forward for centuries.

Amazing companies have arisen here, creating groundbreaking technologies and systems that have greatly advanced society. Such innovation can be applied to many sectors of American life, including helping the homeless, educating those who need it, and improving the lives of workers. The best companies treat employees well and take care of their needs. Let's examine how American innovation can serve society and improve the lives of the people who work and live in this country.

First, American innovation can be applied to helping the homeless. Currently, there are over 500,000 homeless people in the US, and numbers have been rising since 2016.[51] Innovations in low-cost housing and other construction technologies can help us address this issue. Modular construction, 3D printing, and prefabrication can be used to cut costs and construct affordable housing more quickly. Additionally, innovation in new technologies for building energy-efficient homes could reduce energy costs for these homes and make them more accessible to the people who need them most.

Second, better training systems can help American workers even in the highest of high-tech jobs. In July 2023, the Arizona location of the Taiwan Semiconductor Manufacturing Company announced a delay to its plans to begin mass production of a specific line of computer chips solely because of a skilled labor shortage. While America does have an impressive record of innovation, including the actual invention of the microchip, it's clear to see this particular problem could have been prevented had more workers received better training. Innovating not just what we're building but also how we keep our workforce of builders trained will make sure these jobs stay in America.

Third, some of the best companies are defense contractors or military research companies. These companies play a critical role in society by developing technologies and systems that help keep America safe. They also benefit from a well-trained workforce. By treating their employees well and continuing their education, these companies can maintain a skilled and dedicated workforce that can help them remain competitive.

Fourth, innovation in how we teach and train people will benefit America. There are many great American companies that are efficient and are building innovative systems for teaching and learning. With new technology and educational models, we can better prepare our children and anyone who needs further training or retooling their skills for the future. The benefits are many—from reducing student loans to creating better skilled workers. American innovation in education should be encouraged and supported.

American innovation has already made significant contributions to society, and it has the potential to make many more while still keeping the goal of raising the value of our labor intact. From reducing homelessness to better serving workers, to creating breakthroughs in military technology and education, the possibilities are endless.[52] To keep America great, our innovators must continue to create new ideas and technologies that serve the needs of society. By supporting innovation and putting its power to use, we can create a better, more prosperous tomorrow for all Americans, and rather than innovate people out of their jobs, we can innovate them into better situations.

CONCEPT 3: Return to an Asset-backed Currency

Money is a universal concept in the modern world. We use it to buy goods and services, pay rent, and save for the future. But while we frequently handle currency in our daily lives, it can be easy to forget its true significance. Currency is, in many ways, a measure of time and value. It dictates how we are compensated for our work, how much our possessions are worth, how we trade peacefully, and how we pay taxes to our government (and how much we owe if we have a lot of money). Yet the value of currency is not always apparent, and its worth can depend on various factors, including inflation, government policy, and the availability of alternative assets.

We want to look at the complexity of currency, inflation, and the value of money before recommending a way to improve our currency.

Inflation and Its Impact on Currency

Inflation can be a difficult concept to fully understand. At its most basic level, it refers to a decrease in the purchasing power of a currency. When inflation occurs, the cost of goods and services increases, and the value of each unit of currency decreases. This can lead to various economic issues, including reduced consumer spending, increased lending rates, and lower investment returns.

One common question about inflation is why it occurs in the first place. In many cases, it stems from an increase in the money supply within a society. If too much money enters circulation, either through the government printing new bills or increased lending and borrowing, it can lead to a situation where prices rise faster than wages. Inflation can also be caused by external factors, such as a natural disaster or war, that disrupt production and drive up prices.

Historical Approaches to Inflation

Governments throughout history have taken various approaches to reducing inflation. One of the most common methods is to raise interest rates, which can make borrowing more expensive and therefore lower the demand for goods and services. Another approach is to reduce government spending, which can ease the money supply and reduce pressure on prices. Some governments have even implemented price controls and rationing in times of crisis to prevent runaway inflation.

However, there are trade-offs to each of these methods. Raising interest rates can lead to lower investment and slower economic growth. Reducing government spending can potentially harm citizens who rely on government services. And price controls can lead to shortages and black markets. Ultimately, managing inflation requires a delicate balance and deep understanding of the economic and political factors at play.

Since American Laborism is specifically calling for reduced government and government spending, it's important for us to have a stable currency that can handle this newly shrunken spending.

Backing Currency with Valuable Assets

To combat inflation and maintain the value of currency, some societies have tied their currency to assets that possess low inflation. Historically, one of the most popular assets for this purpose has been gold. Because the supply of gold grows slowly and is finite, it can provide a stable foundation for currency. However, gold can be difficult to transport and store, which has led some societies to seek alternative backing assets.

One such asset is bitcoin, a digital currency that has gained popularity in recent years. Bitcoin is decentralized and operates independently of government or financial systems. This makes it resistant to inflation caused by government policies or economic conditions. However, bitcoin is still relatively new, and its value can be volatile.

Other assets considered for currency backing include diamonds and real estate. Diamonds have long been considered a valuable and stable asset, with consistent demand and limited supply. Similarly, real estate has the potential to provide stable backing, as it is a tangible and finite resource. However, real estate can be difficult to manage on a national scale, and values can vary significantly based on location and local economic conditions.

Hope for a Stronger US Dollar

Ultimately, the goal of currency backing is to create a currency that maintains its value over time and remains stable in the face of economic uncertainty. With a combination of the right backing assets, the US dollar could maintain its position as one of the strongest currencies on the planet. However, achieving this goal will require thoughtful and careful policy decisions, as well as a strong understanding of the factors that impact currency value.

Indeed, the value of currency and inflation can be complex and challenging topics to fully grasp. But understanding their impact on our lives and economy is critical to making informed decisions about our future. Backing our currency with valuable, low-inflation assets like gold, bitcoin, diamonds, or real estate can help maintain its value over time. With careful management and a keen eye on both domestic and international economic factors, we have the potential to create a truly strong and stable US dollar.

CONCEPT 4: Build More Schools

Because all federal benefits are tied to training and education, we'll expect to see millions of people wanting to attend school, and we'll need adequate facilities for all of them. Children, teens, adults, and entire families who are eager to continue their education to improve their lives will mean we need to provide the resources they need to do so. Here are potential solutions to address this pressing need for more schools in America and create a brighter future for our communities.

Partnering with Existing Schools

One practical solution for accommodating millions of new students is for the American Laborism federal government Advancement Department to partner with existing elementary, middle, and high schools, colleges and universities, private schools, and even for-profit schools. By doing this, we can share resources, such as buildings, and create evening or weekend schools. This solution is cost-effective and sustainable, as it reduces building costs and maximizes the use of existing facilities.

Using Government Property

Another option is to use the millions of square feet of office space owned or leased by the United States government. While this may not be the perfect use for office real estate, we can leverage these assets to provide much-needed schools in areas where partnering schools might be limited. This is a short-term solution, but it is still viable as we work to reduce the size and cost of government operations, as we'll be divesting of as much real estate as possible.

Leveraging Military Support

US military engineers can also help build or convert schools, just like they do in foreign countries that need support during times of conflict. We can tap into their expertise in construction and use their resources to build new schools or renovate existing ones. This collaboration can extend beyond the military and include partnerships with other industries that can provide financial or logistical support.

Distance Learning and Homeschooling

We can also explore the option of distance learning or homeschooling to provide educational opportunities to more people. With advances in technology, we can leverage devices and internet connectivity to deliver online education and training. Homeschooling is also a viable option, as it provides flexibility and can be tailored to the unique needs of each student. These approaches can be especially useful for people in rural areas and those who may have difficulty accessing traditional classrooms.

If the acceptance and popularity of American Laborism creates high demand for school facilities, that is a pressing issue that needs our immediate attention. We need to create opportunities for more students, both young and old, so they can access education and training to improve their lives. By partnering with existing schools, utilizing government property, leveraging military support, and exploring innovative approaches like distance learning and homeschooling, we can create a brighter future for everyone. It's up to us to invest in education, support our communities, and pave the way for a better world.

CONCEPT 5: Build More Housing

The last piece of the puzzle for how we can make this happen is to answer the question of where all these people seeking benefits will live.

It's a fair question, mostly because very few of us are willing to accept that the federal government we've had until now could adequately house people. The history of public housing in America is filled with terrible stories of dilapidated buildings and substandard homes for people at one end of the spectrum, or phenomenally expensive, overbudget, and behind-schedule housing on the other end.

But if we propose to offer housing—even temporarily—as a benefit, we must solve this. We could see hundreds of thousands, if not millions, of people come to us for housing and meet their half of the bargain to enroll in schools and work at least one day a week.

For one, we won't require people who currently have housing to move out of it in order to collect benefits. As for paying for their rent or mortgage, if they want to stay in that house, that will remain their responsibility. They don't have to move out, but they aren't having the costs covered. However, they will have five days a week to work and earn money to pay for their housing.

For many people, housing is already a major problem across the United States. We need a solution that accommodates them. We need more housing facilities to offer a better living situation for those in need, who apply for school and work.

One possible solution will be to work as partners with existing schools with dormitory or student housing facilities. The benefit is that it can integrate a solution into existing infrastructure and help oil the wheels of the housing and education sectors.

But housing may still be needed in areas that don't have suitable partner schools. In that case, like the last section, we can consider using the federal government's real estate for temporary housing. This allocation of housing facilities through the government can provide people with the basic need for shelter and can even help the US economy by creating jobs and converting these spaces.

Similar to building schools, another possibility is that US military engineers can help build or convert temporary housing, just like they do for soldiers or refugees in times of conflict or natural disaster. The military is skilled at this and can contribute toward the infrastructure of the country, not just in times of war but also in times of peace. Using the expert knowledge of the military to increase housing facilities can prove to be a vital solution to the pressing issue.

Moreover, rather than the well-known failures of governments to provide decent housing for at-need people in the past, such as low-income homes costing millions of dollars to build, initially, our standard will be that "housing good enough for our soldiers is good enough." This means that the same standards used for military housing can be used for temporary civilian housing, which will significantly speed the construction process and improve the quality of housing provided.

And don't forget that people seeking benefits are obligated to contribute labor, some of which can be directed to building housing or refurbishing or repurposing available real estate into housing.

As a result, not just children and teens but even adults who want benefits and don't have adequate housing currently can benefit from the available solutions. The result of these changes in housing facilities could lead to millions of people enrolling in schools, and a corresponding rise in employment, as schools would need more administration and teaching staff. In turn, the expanded education system will lead to innovation, new ideas, and better opportunities, leading to an overall enhancement of society.

A better standard of housing is necessary for millions of people across the US. The lack of adequate housing facilities often hinders individuals from accessing education and better job prospects. We need to develop a framework that facilitates the integration of housing and education infrastructure. The US government can help with temporary housing, the military can help build or convert temporary housing, and partnerships with private educational institutions can enhance the process. By using the same standards of military housing for civilian housing, we can significantly speed up the process of building decent housing and create more opportunities for millions of people. In doing so, we work together toward a brighter future.

CHAPTER 15

REDUCING GOVERNMENT SOLVES AMERICA VS. AMERICANS

IT'S TIME TO GET to work showing how small government solves "American vs. Americans." An expected criticism of American Laborism is, "How can you possibly reduce the entire executive branch of the federal government to just three departments? What about the [fill in the blank] department?"

That's because our government has grown so big with so many people working on so many different things that they don't serve us as well as they might, so it can be hard to imagine smart, innovative, educated Americans not needing such a big government.

For example, investors might immediately wonder how they'd survive and prosper without the Securities and Exchange Commission (SEC)? Armed with a set of laws generated in 1933, 1934, and 1940, and supposedly charged with protecting investors, does the SEC have a place in a reduced-size government?

Before we answer that, we'd like to clarify that the SEC, as an independent agency created by Congress, isn't part of the executive branch and wouldn't automatically be eliminated by American Laborism. That makes the SEC an interesting case study, as we're contemplating reducing virtually everything around them, including the Department of Justice (DOJ), with whom the SEC works closely when their civil investigations warrant criminal charges that the DOJ can prosecute.

But the SEC's five commissioners are appointed by the US president, who sits atop the executive branch. Therefore, a president overseeing America's conversion to American Laborism and cutting executive branch departments could easily fill the SEC's five leadership seats with people who want to reduce it in coordination with the rest of the executive branch.

You might think cutting such a high-profile department as the SEC will put investors at risk. But without going into specifics, the truth is, even with a fully funded SEC, investors still lose money.

The SEC didn't protect investors from the Enron, Long-Term Capital Management, WorldCom, Lehman Brothers, General Motors, Conseco, or Chrysler bankruptcies.

If the SEC had a flawless track record of helping investors and preventing fraud and bad investments, the case against shrinking them would be better. It would be generous to say the SEC might sometimes protect investors from tiny amounts of fraud and scams. Perhaps. But they, by no means, prevent fraud and scams from happening and hurting investors. In fact, you could argue that the SEC often acts after the damage is done, rarely in time to prevent investors from losing money.

But think about this: what if the key to helping investors is to advance their education? Wouldn't it be possible, in a federal government that leans so heavily on advancing education, to teach Americans how to invest? If we wanted to, we could even create a certification process that mandated someone had taken and passed a basic investing course before they were cleared for investing.

Do you see how focusing on education might change how Americans approach investing?

There are two more valuable aspects of this to consider.

First, every company or organization in America either has to register or incorporate within a specific state, or opt out. That means each state is already responsible for maintaining their own rules for what it takes to incorporate or organize, and they can just as easily require reporting of offering shares or tokens to investors if they aren't already.

Second, Americans aren't well served by the current state of regulating possible investments. This could be a book all its own, but here are two brief examples. First, to "protect" investors, many possible investments are only available to people who pass a criterion known as an *accredited investor*. This is a device that allows rich people to invest in certain offerings. To become an accredited investor, you need to prove a net worth of $1 million or income of $200,000 ($300,000 combined income if you're married). Granted, in 2020, the SEC expanded the definition of *accredited investor* to include certain categories of investment professionals who may have sufficient knowledge but insufficient income or net worth.

Even so, the expansion to include some people based on their knowledge doesn't extend outside the category of investment professionals. That means a person could profitably manage a business for four decades and still not be considered knowledgeable enough to invest in their own industry if doing so required being an accredited investor!

We don't think that makes any sense.

Plus, if the SEC could fine or sanction organizations that allow Americans to invest, those organizations might just stay privately held or offshore, keeping Americans from investing in them at all.

This is literally an example of America vs. Americans. If an organization attempting to raise money that could become lucrative for investors is forced to exclude Americans, thanks to American laws and their possible enforcement, Americans could be left out of good opportunities.

It's not just about making money, either! Consider the transformative innovations and technologies that are being worked on right now that their inventor or founder will seek to incubate and launch somewhere besides America, because—while we're supposedly capitalists and have a supposedly free market—our laws lead them to launch offshore or in a more friendly jurisdiction.

So yes, when we say we'd be willing to consider reducing the SEC to a combination of investor education and states' rights, we believe we'd be better off doing so!

That was just one example, of course. It makes sense that anyone reading this might pick other departments of the federal government that they can't see themselves doing without. Think about it—there are dozens of departments with hundreds (if not thousands) of bureaucracies they oversee. Obviously, reducing the government drastically, as we propose, is bound to raise questions about cutting something that—at first glance—seems important enough to keep.

We're not saying that life won't change with these cuts. Far from it! What we're saying is Americans can handle the changes.

In fact, you might think an economic system known as America Laborism would require us to keep the US Department of Labor. Hardly. First and foremost, one of the biggest things the Labor Department does is oversee the unemployment programs in partnership with states.

Since American Laborism eliminates cash or monetary unemployment payments and replaces them with in-kind benefits, that program will immediately cease.

But the Department of Labor does more than that, right? Yes, it prosecutes labor and compensation disputes. But this can be done at the state level, since every state can make its own laws about wages, compensation, and fair employee treatment. Plus, by eliminating the bureaucracy of unemployment, states can allocate more resources to ensure that people who are working are treated well, and they can prosecute any employer who mistreats employees.

Plus, with the generous safety net we're offering, you might imagine that people who previously felt trapped in working unsatisfactory jobs could quit, pursue more education or training, and then get a better job.

One more thing the Department of Labor offers the American people is the Occupational Safety and Health Administration (OSHA). OSHA is charged with maintaining rules, laws, and standards that keep employees safe. As such, it *sounds* important and not something we'd want to cut.

Except we have to question how effective OSHA actually is. The American insurance industry estimates that there are as many as 4.9 million workers' compensation claims for on-the-job injuries every year.[53] That tells us OSHA isn't protecting everyone.

Perhaps using the same framework we did for the SEC, we could better protect employees with increased state involvement and increased training and education—something American Laborism is perfectly designed to do. And remember, every company with employees in America must be registered with a state. Therefore, the jurisdiction of keeping employees safe can likely be better served by state officials closer to the problem, rather than Washington, DC, bureaucrats who aren't.

We've given two examples of current US government agencies or departments and how they can be effectively replaced with increased state involvement and better education and training of the American people. While most departments and agencies probably have one or two critical missions that are beneficial to the American people, they've mostly all grown into huge bureaucracies that perform nine unneeded functions for each one valid function. That means it won't be hard to reassign the core responsibility and cancel the rest.

If we do, we get a country that can pay off its debts while raising the standard of living for everyone. We can reduce the instances of America working against the interests of Americans. We can eliminate involuntary poverty and homelessness.

Say goodbye to big, unnecessary government propped up by unnecessarily high taxes.

Say goodbye to capitalism.

Say hello to American Laborism. We can make America a better place.

ACKNOWLEDGMENTS

Eric

I would like to first and foremost acknowledge my wife, Ana, without whom this book would likely still be just an idea in a dusty corner of my mind. Ana's support, curiosity, drive, and energy are priceless. Before the first word of this book was written, Ana saw the potential to improve people's lives and America, too, from the first idea that would grow to become what it is today. Thank you, Ana, for believing I could do this.

To my mother and father, brothers, and sister, who have always let me talk through whatever is on my mind, giving me a tailwind or a contradiction as needed.

To all of my research and publishing colleagues at Stansberry Research, who indulged me with jokes, debates, and brainstorming about ideas. Specifically: Stephen, who adds creativity to every idea; Andrew, who sharpens every point; John, who understands innovation better than anyone; Lisa, Fawn, and Andreea, who know what I meant to say; Kelly, who creates brilliant stories; Michael, who sees the future; Matt, for watching out for me; Brett, who listens; and to Kim, who saw the writer in me. And I would also like to make a special acknowledgment to the most important part of my writing, the adventuresome folks who take my letters and give my work meaning.

Last, I would like to acknowledge Professor Philip Ganderton, whose economics lectures left a lifelong impression.

Phil

I would like to express my heartfelt gratitude to my wonderful wife for her unwavering support and love. To my family, thank you for your constant encouragement and belief in me. And last, to Satoshi Nakamoto, whose groundbreaking work in the field of cryptocurrency has paved the way for a new era of financial innovation and freedom. Thank you all for being an essential part of my life, shaping my path, and enriching my experiences.

ENDNOTES

1. Charlotte Jee, "AI Will Disrupt White-Collar Workers the Most, Predicts a New Report," MIT Technology Review, November 20, 2019, https://www.technology review.com/2019/11/20/131884/ai-will-disrupt-white-collar-workers-the-most -predicts-a-new-report.

2. Jee, "AI Will Disrupt White-Collar Workers the Most."

3. "Consumer Price Index for All Urban Consumers: Purchasing Power of the Consumer Dollar in U.S. City Average," FRED, August 10, 2023, https://fred.stlouisfed.org/series/CUUR0000SA0R.

4. "OIG Oversight of the Unemployment Insurance Program," United States Department of Labor, updated June 8, 2023, https://www.oig.dol.gov/doloiguioversightwork.htm.

5. Jaclyn Diaz, "Michigan Paid Up to $8.5 Billion in Fraudulent Jobless Claims During the Pandemic," NPR, December 30, 2021, https://www.npr.org /2021/12/30/1069048017/michigan-paid-8-5-billion-in-fraudulent-jobless -claims-during-the-pandemic.

6. "Chinese Military Personnel Charged with Computer Fraud, Economic Espionage and Wire Fraud for Hacking into Credit Reporting Agency Equifax," Office of Public Affairs, February 10, 2020, https://www.justice.gov/opa/pr/chinese-military -personnel-charged-computer-fraud-economic-espionage-and-wire-fraud-hacking.

7. "DOL-OIG Oversight of the Unemployment Insurance Program," *Revised Pandemic Response Oversight Plan*, June 30, 2023, https://www.oig.dol.gov/OIG_Pandemic _Response_Portal.htm.

8. Eric Boehm, "Over $400 Billion in COVID Aid Was Stolen or Wasted," Reason.com, June 14, 2023, https://reason.com/2023/06/14/over-400-billion-in-covid-aid-was -stolen-or-wasted.

9. Linley Sanders, "Americans Believe Benefits Fraud Is Common for SNAP," YouGov, September 10, 2019, https://today.yougov.com/topics/politics/articles -reports/2019/09/10/benefits-fraud-common-survey.

10. Sanders, "Americans Believe Benefits Fraud Is Common for SNAP."

11. Tanya Lewis, "The U.S. Just Lost 26 Years' Worth of Progress on Life Expectancy," *Scientific American,* October 17, 2022, https://www.scientificamerican.com/article /the-u-s-just-lost-26-years-worth-of-progress-on-life-expectancy.

12. D. McCarty et al., "Alcoholism, Drug Abuse, and the Homeless," *American Psychologist* 46, no. 11 (November 1991): 1139-48, https://pubmed.ncbi.nlm.nih.gov/1772151.

13. "Homelessness and Addiction," Addiction Center, September 4, 2023, https://www.addictioncenter.com/addiction/homelessness.

14. United States Interagency Council on Homelessness, https://www.usich.gov/tools-for-action/map.

15. US Department of Health and Human Services, https://www.hhs.gov/programs/social-services/homelessness/research/index.html.

16. Isabel V. Sawhill, "Poverty in America," Econlib.com, https://www.econlib.org/library/Enc/PovertyinAmerica.html.

17. Adam Michel, "In 1 Chart, How Much the Rich Pay in Taxes," Heritage Foundation, March 3, 2021, https://www.heritage.org/taxes/commentary/1-chart-how-much-the-rich-pay-taxes.

18. Budget of the United States Government, Fiscal Year 2023 (whitehouse.gov)

19. "Total Household Debt Reaches $16.90 trillion in Q4 2022; Mortgage and Auto Loan Growth Slows," press release, Federal Reserve Bank of New York, February 16, 2023, newyorkfed.org.

20. Amy Howe, "Supreme Court Strikes Down Biden Student-Loan Forgiveness Program," *SCOTUSblog*, June 30, 2023, https://www.scotusblog.com/2023/06/supreme-court-strikes-down-biden-student-loan-forgiveness-program/.

21. Govind Bhutada, "The Rising Cost of College in the US," Visual Capitalist, February 3, 2021, https://www.visualcapitalist.com/rising-cost-of-college-in-u-s/.

22. "Education Pays, 2022," US Bureau of Labor Statistics, May 2023, https://www.bls.gov/careeroutlook/2023/data-on-display/education-pays.htm.

23. "NEWS: Sanders, Grassley and Colleagues Make Bipartisan Push to Audit the Pentagon and End Wasteful Spending," Senator Bernie Sanders, June 21, 2023, https://www.sanders.senate.gov/press-releases/news-sanders-grassley-and-colleagues-make-bipartisan-push-to-audit-the-pentagon-and-end-wasteful-spending/.

24. "Comer & Sessions Open Probe into Department of Defense After Failing GAO Audit for Fifth Time," Committee on Oversight and Accountability, press release, March 6, 2023, https://oversight.house.gov/release/comer-sessions-open-probe-into-department-of-defense-after-failing-gao-audit-for-fifth-time.

25. Katelyn Brown, "Tax Code Is So Long that Nobody's Really Sure of Its Length," Politifact, October 17, 2017, https://www.politifact.com/factchecks/2017/oct/17/roy-blunt/tax-code-so-long-nobodys-really-sure-its-length.

26. "Distributional Analysis of the U.S. Tax System," U.S. Department of the Treasury, https://home.treasury.gov/policy-issues/tax-policy/office-of-tax-analysis.

27. "Households and Nonprofit Organizations; Net Worth, Level," FRED, June 8, 2023, stlouisfed.org.

28. Julia F. Irwin, "The Origins of U.S. Foreign Disaster Assistance," Organization of American Historians, oah.org.

29. Gay & Fisher, "The Commission for Relief in Belgium, 1929," chapter 4, sections 1-2, byu.edu.

30. "United Nations Relief and Rehabilitation Administration," Holocaust Encyclopedia, https://encyclopedia.ushmm.org/content/en/article/united-nations-relief-and-rehabilitation-administration.

31. "Marshall Plan (1948)," National Archives, https://www.archives.gov/milestone-documents/marshall-plan.

32. Dashboard, ForeignAssistance.gov.

33. *2020 USCIS Statistical Annual Report*, PDF, USCIS.gov.

34. Andrea Peer, "Global Poverty: Facts, FAQs, and How to Help," World Vision, updated April 4, 2023, https://www.worldvision.org/sponsorship-news-stories/global-poverty-facts#facts.

35. Richard V. Reeves, Katherine Guyot, and Eleanor Krause, "A Dozen Ways to Be Middle Class," Brookings, May 8, 2018, https://www.brookings.edu/articles/a-dozen-ways-to-be-middle-class/.

36. "Quick Facts," United States Census Bureau, https://www.census.gov/quickfacts/fact/table/US/PST045222.

37. "Census Bureau Median Family Income By Family Size," Justice.gov, https://www.justice.gov/ust/eo/bapcpa/20220401/bci_data/median_income_table.htm.

38. "Annual Earnings by Educational Attainment," National Center for Education Statistics, May 2023, https://nces.ed.gov/programs/coe/indicator/cba.

39. Emily Dohrman and Bruce Fallick, "Is the Middle Class Worse Off Than It Used to Be?" Federal Reserve Bank of Cleveland, February 12, 2020, https://www.cleveland-fed.org/publications/economic-commentary/2020/ec-202003-is-middle-class-worse-off.

40. ATTOM Team, "U.S. Foreclosure Activity Sees Spike in May 2023," ATTOM, June 8, 2023, https://www.attomdata.com/news/market-trends/foreclosures/attom-may-2023-u-s-foreclosure-market-report.

41. "Bankruptcy Filings Drop 6.3 Percent," United States Courts, February 6, 2023, https://www.uscourts.gov/news/2023/02/06/bankruptcy-filings-drop-63-percent#.

42. Mark Webb, "Delinquent Car Loans, Repossessions Are Rising In America: Report," motor1.com, April 25, 2023, https://www.motor1.com/news/664132/delinquent-car-loans-repos-rising/#.

43. "Charge-Off and Delinquency Rates on Loans and Leases at Commercial Banks," Federal Reserve System, https://www.federalreserve.gov/releases/chargeoff/delallsa.htm.

44. Matthew McGough et al., "How Does Health Spending in the U.S. Compare to Other Countries?" Health System Tracker, February 9, 2023, https://www.healthsystemtracker.org/chart-collection/health-spending-u-s-compare-countries/#Per%20capita%20health%20consumption%20expenditures,%20U.S.%20dollars,%20PPP%20adjusted,%202020%20and%202021.

45. Lorie Konish, "This Is the Real Reason Most Americans File for Bankruptcy," CNBC, February 11, 2019, https://www.cnbc.com/2019/02/11/this-is-the-real-reason-most-americans-file-for-bankruptcy.html.

46. Salvador Rizzo, "Sanders's Flawed Statistic: 500,000 Medical Bankruptcies a Year," *Washington Post*, August 28, 2019, https://www.washingtonpost.com/politics/2019/08/28/sanderss-flawed-statistic-medical-bankruptcies-year/.

47. Ryan Nunn, Jana Parsons, and Jay Shambaugh, "A Dozen Facts About the Economics of the US Health-care System," Brookings, March 10, 2020, https://www.brookings.edu/articles/a-dozen-facts-about-the-economics-of-the-u-s-health-care-system.

48. Jay Bhattacharya and Neeraj Sood, "Who Pays for Obesity?" *Journal of Economic Perspectives* 25, no. 1 (Winter 2011): 139-58, https://www.ncbi.nlm.nih.gov/pmc/articles/PMC6415902.

49. Janet M. Corrigan, Jill Eden, and Barbara M. Smith, eds., Per the URL https://nap.nationalacademies.org/catalog/10537/leadership-by-example-coordinating-government-roles-in-improving-health-care *Leadership by Example: Coordinating Government Roles in Improving Health Care Quality*, chapter 2, "Overview of the Government Health Care Programs," (National Academies Press, 2003); Stephen Moore, "8 Reasons to Still Hate Obamacare," Heritage Foundation, June 5, 2018, https://www.heritage.org/health-care-reform/commentary/8-reasons-still-hate-obamacare.

50. Lydia Saad, "Americans Sour on U.S. Healthcare Quality," Gallup, January 19, 2023, https://news.gallup.com/poll/468176/americans-sour-healthcare-quality.aspx.

51. Tanya de Sousa et al., "The 2022 Annual Homelessness Assessment Report (AHAR) to Congress, Part 1: Point-In-Time Estimates of Homelessness, December 2022," huduser.gov, https://www.huduser.gov/portal/sites/default/files/pdf/2022-ahar-part-1.pdf.

52. I write about many of them here: Stansberry Research, https://stansberryresearch.com/products/stansberry-innovations-report.

53. Sa El, "How Many Workers Comp Claims Happen Per Year? Plus Over 27 Workers Compensation Statistics For Sep 2023!" Simply Insurance, February 4, 2023, https://www.simplyinsurance.com/how-many-workers-comp-claims-per-year/.

ABOUT THE
AUTHORS

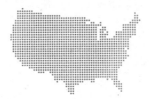

ERIC WADE is the editor of Stansberry Research's three cryptocurrency investment advisories, which have created millionaires and changed people's lives. Eric made Internet history selling the first domain name (Wallstreet.com) for over $1 million, sold a movie script to actor Adam Sandler, and founded a Los Angeles music business that was recognized locally and internationally. Studying economics in college fueled his desire to remake capitalism, reshape our government, reduce taxes, and improve the standard of living for all Americans. Eric lives in California with Ana, his wife of thirty-two years, who is a children's book author and inspiration for his big ideas.

PHIL HEREL, a New York native, holds a doctorate in physical therapy from Stony Brook University and a bachelor of science in biology from SUNY Oneonta. He owns a successful outpatient physical therapy clinic in California, specializing in orthopedic and neurological ailments. Phil advocates for healthcare system improvements and envisions a more equitable future with reduced taxes, economic growth, and improved living standards. Phil is a knowledgeable investor in stocks and cryptocurrencies, actively participating in crypto activities such as staking and mining. Phil shares his life with his talented wife, Monica, who is a singer-songwriter and fitness trainer. They continually motivate and drive each other to excel in their pursuits.